T0289438

TEXAS TURTLES & CROCODILIANS

TEXAS NATURAL HISTORY GUIDES™

TEXAS TURTLES
& CROCODILIANS

A FIELD GUIDE

TROY D. HIBBITTS
AND TERRY L. HIBBITTS

UNIVERSITY OF TEXAS PRESS
Austin

Unless otherwise indicated, all photos were taken by the authors.

Requests for permission to reproduce material from this work should be sent to:

Permissions
University of Texas Press
P.O. Box 7819
Austin, TX 78713-7819
http://utpress.utexas.edu/index.php/rp-form

♾ The paper used in this book meets the minimum requirements of ANSI/NISO Z39.48-1992 (R1997) (Permanence of Paper).

LIBRARY OF CONGRESS CATALOGING-IN-PUBLICATION DATA

Hibbitts, Troy D., 1970– author.
    Texas turtles & crocodilians : a field guide / Troy D. Hibbitts and Terry L. Hibbitts. — First edition.
        pages   cm —   (Texas natural history guides)
    Includes bibliographical references and index.
    ISBN 978-1-4773-0777-9 (pbk. : alk. paper)
    ISBN 978-1-4773-0861-5 (library e-book)
    ISBN 978-1-4773-0862-2 (non-library e-book)
    1. Turtles—Texas—Identification.   2. Crocodilians—Texas—Identification.   I. Hibbitts, Terry L., author.   II. Title.   III. Title: Texas turtles and crocodilians.   IV. Series : Texas natural history guides.
    QL666.C5H525   2016
    597.9209764—dc23   2015015678

doi: 10.7560/307779

We dedicate this book to the late Martin Ernest Jarrell, who maintained his son-in-law, Terry's, box turtle collection in his backyard from the time Terry went off to college in 1966 until 1991. This colony of box turtles provided a constant source of enjoyment for him and his grandchildren (Troy among them); created fond memories of turtles with names like Hungry, Big Black, Big Brown, Yellowneck, Spotty-Dotty, and Lil'Bit; resulted in numerous natural history observations; and sparked a love of turtles in all who had the opportunity to explore his backyard habitat.

CONTENTS

Contents

FOREWORD

In 1857, just a dozen years after Texas joined the United States, the Swiss-born geologist, naturalist, and Harvard professor Louis Agassiz published a book that attempted to list and describe all the turtles native to North America. It included the first scientific descriptions of two new turtles based on specimens from Texas. The Yellow Mud Turtle (*Kinosternon flavescens*) was described based on several specimens, including one from the Blanco River. The description of the Texas Tortoise (*Gopherus berlandieri*) was based on a specimen from around Brownsville that Agassiz believed had been collected by the French-born, but long-time Mexico resident, Jean Louis Berlandier. For this reason Agassiz named the new tortoise after the Matamoros naturalist and doctor.

The latest turtle to be described based on Texas specimens is Cagle's Map Turtle (*Graptemys caglei*) in 1974. (While it is obvious that the Rio Grande Cooter [*Pseudemys gorzugi*], described in 1984, is primarily a Texas turtle, the type specimen was collected across the river in Coahuila.) In the 117 years between

1857 and 1974 about another half dozen turtles have been officially described based on specimens collected in Texas.

Over the years there have been many scientific books on reptiles and amphibians, covering both North America and individual states. The earliest attempts to summarize the herpetological knowledge for the United States were in the 1820s by Richard Harlan and a decade later by John Holbrook. At the time, of course, Texas was not a part of the United States. The major books devoted to our understanding of all US turtles are works by Louis Agassiz in 1857, Clifford Pope in 1939, Archie Carr in 1952, Carl Ernst and Roger Barbour in 1972, and Ernst and Jeff Lovich in 2009. Publications attempting to at least list all the reptiles and amphibians in Texas begin with John Strecker's 1915 *Reptiles and Amphibians of Texas*. Bryce Brown significantly updated the list with both new discoveries and specific locality data in 1950, and Gerald Raun and Frederick Gehlbach added range maps and a bibliography of all scientific publications that involved Texas reptiles and amphibians to their 1972 revision of Brown's work. James R. Dixon continued the use of county-specific range maps and greatly expanded the bibliography in his 1987 *Amphibians and Reptiles of Texas*, the latest revision of which was published in 2013. There have been a few publications devoted to one group of Texas reptiles (okay, snakes), but until 2012's *Texas Amphibians* by the late Bob Tipton and colleagues, no book was devoted to a single group other than snakes. Which brings us to the present volume (I'm ignoring the fact that it also includes Texas's single crocodilian, the alligator).

This current treatment is long overdue. The Texas turtle fauna is large and diverse. It includes forms that are found nowhere else, Cagle's Map Turtle (*Graptemys caglei*) and the Texas Map Turtle (*Graptemys versa*), and wide-ranging species that barely touch the state, like the Painted Turtle (*Chrysemys picta*) and the Rough-footed Mud Turtle (*Kinosternon hirtipes*). In addition to accounts of individual species that summarize our current knowledge of these ancient and fascinating animals, the book includes an overview of their evolution and position within the lineage of vertebrates and a description of their natural history. This information is augmented by suggestions about observing and photographing these reptiles in their natural habitat and, if collected, how to maintain them properly in captivity. Since most of the subjects of this book live in freshwater, a very useful discussion of the state's river systems is included. A dichotomous key is provided but is probably unnecessary in most cases because the excellent photographs and descriptions in the text will surely be sufficient to identify almost any specimen.

There is often some friendly contention about who is the "Dean of Texas Herpetology" at any particular time. However I maintain that at this time, and for the last decade at least and for the foreseeable future, there is no confusion over who is the premier family of Texas herpetologists. I have known Terry Hibbitts for about 50 years and have watched as he and his sons, Toby and Troy, have excelled in herpetological field work, animal photography, academic endeavors, teaching, and now publishing. All three have been members of the Texas Herpetological Society for decades, and all three have served as officers of the society, including president. I've seen their spouses, children, and grandchildren at field meetings and symposia. No one, in my view, is more qualified to produce this book.

DAVID HAYNES
SAN ANTONIO, 2014

ACKNOWLEDGMENTS

We would like to express special thanks to our wives—Marla and Diana Hibbitts—and to our daughter and granddaughter—Cheyenne Hibbitts—and our brother and son—Toby Hibbitts—who have long supported and continue to support our interest in nature, especially reptiles and amphibians, which led to this book. Thanks is also necessary for their constant support during this project as they allowed us to devote substantial amounts of time, at home, on the road, and in the field, to the writing and the collection of photographs for this book.

Both of us are lifelong members of the Texas Herpetological Society (THS) and have attended THS spring field meets, beginning in the late 1960s for Terry and the mid-1970s for Troy. The THS was instrumental in fostering our interest in the field of herpetology and herpetological natural history. As a society, the THS serves as a bridge between amateur and professional herpetologists in Texas and fosters genuine discussion and discourse between these two groups.

We would like to thank the various professors of herpetology who have guided our education: the late James R. Dixon, Professor Emeritus in the Wildlife and Fisheries Department at Texas A&M University; Jonathan A. Campbell, Biology Department Chair at the University of Texas at Arlington; the late Richard Baldauf, Professor in the Wildlife and Fisheries Department at Texas A&M; Donald Clark, Professor in the Wildlife and Fisheries Department at Texas A&M; and the late Donald Ingold, Professor at East Texas State University (now Texas A&M University—Commerce). Each of these individuals contributed greatly and directly to our education in herpetology, as well as acting as mentors and friends.

Toby Hibbitts' assistance in searching academic references through the Texas A&M University library system was crucial throughout the drafting of this volume.

We would like to thank our reviewers Robert Hansen and Peter V. Lindeman whose suggestions were invaluable in getting the manuscript for this book ready for print. Casey Kittrell at the University of Texas Press was an eager advocate for our work and was instrumental in paving the way for the publication of this volume.

Additional photographs for this book were contributed by Bryan Box, Carl Buttner, Mallory Fontenot, Tony Galluci, Dan Hershman, Marla Hibbitts, Toby Hibbitts, Bill Love at Blue Chameleon Ventures, William Mertz, William B. Montgomery, Mike Pingleton, Michael Price, Sal Scibetta, Michael A. Smith, John T. Williams, Kenneth P. Wray, and the National Park Service-Padre Island National Seashore. Without their contributions, this work would be incompletely illustrated and substantially less useful as a field guide.

TEXAS TURTLES & CROCODILIANS

INTRODUCTION

WHAT IS A TURTLE?

Turtles are a unique and easily recognized group of four-legged, amniotic vertebrates that possess a specialized shell composed of bone or bone and cartilage and which evolved from the bones of their ribs, spine, and sternum. Turtles are unique in that both their shoulder and pelvic girdles are contained *inside* their rib cage (the modified ribs represented by their shells). In most turtles, the shell is made of hardened dermal bone and covered in horny scutes composed primarily of keratin. The shell provides these turtles with protection from most predators. In a few highly aquatic, strong-swimming species, as well as one crevice-dwelling species, the bone of the shell is largely replaced with cartilage. In such species, the bone of the shell has been lost, either to facilitate swimming or to allow the turtle to squeeze into tight crevices. All living turtles lack teeth, and their mouths are bordered by a keratin-lined beak supported by a hard ridge of bone.

Evolutionary History

The oldest fossil turtles date from 220 million years ago, making turtles an older lineage than all other living tetrapods except for the synapsid groups that gave rise to the mammals. The earliest turtle fossils include *Odontochelys semitestacea*, which possessed a complete carapace and incomplete plastron, similar to the condition seen in some stages of embryonic development of modern turtles. More recent fossils had a complete plastron, indicating that this successful and unique anatomical feature (the shell) has been present in essentially its modern form for a very long time indeed. By this measure, the turtle's body plan of possessing an armored shell indicates that it is one of evolution's great success stories.

Two Main Turtle Groups

Modern turtles are divided into two main groups, the Pleurodira, or side-necked turtles, and the Cryptodira, or hidden-necked turtles. The Pleurodira is thought to be the more primitive group, and members withdraw their heads sideways, only partially protecting the head under the margins of the carapace. The Pleurodira includes 79 species of freshwater turtles

Pelomedusa subrufra, South Africa. A typical side-necked turtle. Photo by Toby J. Hibbitts.

Trachemys scripta, Hidalgo Co., Texas. A typical hidden-necked turtle.

occurring primarily in South America, Africa, and Austra-
lia. Although the Pleurodira is considered by most biologists
to be more primitive than the Cryptodira, the oldest fossils
are 50 million years younger than the oldest known Cryptodira fossils, dating from the late Cretaceous around 140 million
years ago.

The Cryptodira includes those turtles that withdraw their
heads and necks directly back into their shells. Most turtle species familiar to Texans are members of this group, including sea
turtles, tortoises, and most freshwater turtles. There are 248 species in this group, and they occur on all continents save Antarctica as well as in all tropical and warm temperate oceans.
The oldest Cryptodira fossils date to the late Jurassic around
190 million years ago.

Relationship between Turtles and Other "Reptiles"

Formerly, the class Reptilia included lizards, snakes, amphisbaenians, the tuatara, turtles, and crocodilians, along with extinct species such as the dinosaurs. However, this classification excluded a closely related specialized group, the birds, and
rather than being united by specialized traits the Reptilia were

instead grouped together based on primitive traits. To correct this situation and for the taxonomy to express the evolutionary relationships among these groups more clearly, a new arrangement was necessary.

Primitively, early amniotic tetrapods—those animals possessing four limbs and laying shelled eggs possessing four membranes around the embryo—can be divided into three groups based upon skull types: anapsid, synapsid, and diapsid. Anapsid skulls possessed a complete roof of dermal bone, synapsid skulls possessed a roof of dermal bone with a single opening present between the temporal and squamosal bone, and diapsid skulls possessed a dermal roof interrupted by two temporal openings, one above and one below the temporal bone. Living animals descending from synapsid reptiles include modern mammals. Living animals likely descending from anapsid reptiles include the turtles, and descendants of the diapsids include lizards, snakes, crocodilians, and birds.

While living turtles clearly possess anapsid skulls, lacking in temporal openings, recent genetic evidence suggests that they may be more closely related to diapsids than to extinct anapsids. However, the data available are conflicting, with some analyses placing the turtles closer to the lizards, snakes, and allies while others place them closer to the archosaurs, including crocodilians and birds. In these analyses, the presence of the anapsid skull in turtles is considered likely to represent a reversion from the diapsid condition. Regardless of which arrangement ultimately proves to be most well supported, the turtles have long been a distinct lineage, with genetic evidence suggesting a divergence at least 255 million years ago.

WHAT IS A CROCODILIAN?

Modern crocodilians are large, four-limbed, tailed, semi-aquatic tetrapod vertebrates with thick armored skins. Although very capable of movement on land, the vast majority of their lives are spent in or near water. All crocodilians are predators and prey on a wide variety of invertebrate and vertebrate prey, with some species specializing in fish while others may specialize in hunting large mammals from ambush. Living crocodilians are largely confined to tropical, subtropical, or warm temperate regions. Crocodilians have diapsid skulls, with two temporal openings, a trait shared with the ancestors of reptiles (lizards, snakes, and relatives), the extinct dinosaurs, and the ancestors of modern birds. With dinosaurs and birds, they are collectively classified as archosaurs (the "Ruling Reptiles").

Evolutionary History

Shortly after the first archosaur fossils appeared in the fossil record but before they underwent the adaptive radiation that gave rise to the dinosaurs, terrestrial crocodilians evolved. The oldest fossils clearly identifiable as crocodilians are about 200 million years old. Crocodilians were probably terrestrial for at least 20 million years before they invaded aquatic habitats. Early crocodilians were divided into a variety of groups, including the Protosuchia, the Sphenosuchia, the Mesosuchia, and the Eusuchia. Of these, the mesosuchians were the largest group of early crocodilians and included both terrestrial and marine forms, with marine forms specialized for near complete aquatic life, possessing limbs modified as flippers and a tail possessing flattened flukes. Most mesosuchians became extinct at the end of the Cretaceous period along with the dinosaurs.

In contrast, all living crocodilians are members of the Eusuchia, a group of primarily semi-aquatic predators that first appeared in the fossil record 120 million years ago. Throughout the fossil record, this successful group has been extremely conservative, with extinct forms appearing morphologically very similar to living species.

Three Main Crocodilian Groups

Modern crocodilians are divided into three families, the Crocodylidae, the Alligatoridae, and the Gavialidae. These groups are separated from one another by approximately 60 million years of evolutionary history, having evolved shortly after the extinction of the dinosaurs in the early Tertiary period.

The Crocodylidae, or "true" crocodiles, possess relatively narrow snouts that are constricted near the tip. With closed jaws, the enlarged fourth tooth of the lower jaw rests in a notch in the upper jaw and is clearly visible. Many of the true crocodiles are noted ambush predators feeding on terrestrial mam-

Crocodylus niloticus, South Africa. A typical crocodile. Photo by Toby J. Hibbitts.

Alligator mississippiensis, Dade Co., Florida. A typical alligator.

mals. There are 16 living species of crocodile arranged in 4 genera: *Crocodylus*, *Mecistops*, *Osteolaemus*, and *Tomistoma*.

The Alligatoridae includes 8 species classified in 4 genera: *Alligator*, *Caiman*, *Melanosuchus*, and *Paleosuchus*. As a group, they are broad-snouted, with all of the teeth of the lower jaw fitting into sockets in the upper jaw when the mouth is closed. Although terrestrial prey such as deer may be occasionally eaten, fish, turtles, and other aquatic vertebrates make up the bulk of the diets of most alligators and caimans.

The Gavialidae includes a single species, the Gharial (*Gavialis gangeticus*). This giant fish-eating animal possesses a greatly elongated, narrow snout—an adaptation common to some aquatic species that feed primarily on small- to medium-sized fish.

Relationship between Crocodilians and Other "Reptiles"

As discussed above, the class Reptilia formerly included lizards, snakes, amphisbaenians, the tuatara, turtles, and crocodilians, along with extinct species such as the dinosaurs. For the taxonomy to express more clearly the evolutionary relationships among these groups, a new arrangement was necessary.

Amniotic tetrapods can be grouped into three categories: anapsid, synapsid, and diapsid. Turtles are considered to be anapsids, mammals are descended from synapsids, and the diapsids include lizards, snakes, crocodilians, and birds.

The diapsid group is, in turn, divided into two basic groups: the Lepidosauria (which includes those animals possessing bodies covered with small scales, including modern lizards, snakes, amphisbaenians, and the tuatara) and the Archosauria (which includes crocodilians and birds). Today, the use of the name Reptilia is typically restricted to modern lepidosaurian animals, whereas living archosaurs are divided into two classes, the Crocodilia and the Aves.

Relationship between Crocodilians and Birds

While birds and crocodilians are each other's closest living relatives, they are separated from one another by at least 200 million years of evolutionary history. Crocodilians and the archosaur lineages that gave rise to the dinosaurs diverged early in the evolutionary history of the archosaurs. Living crocodilians descended from specialized aquatic eusuchian crocodilians, whereas modern birds descended from specialized therapod dinosaurs. While both groups are clearly highly specialized for completely different lifestyles, their affinities can be seen in their scalation as each possesses very similar platelike scales—

in crocodilians covering their entire bodies, while in birds covering only their hind legs.

NATURAL HISTORY
Activity and Seasonality

Most turtle activity (with the notable exception of some mud and musk turtles) occurs during the day when heat from the sun is available to stimulate their activity. Crocodilian activity can be both diurnal and nocturnal, usually depending upon temperatures. Although they are ectothermic, turtles and crocodilians are able to control their body temperatures behaviorally. On a cool, sunny morning, turtles and crocodilians can frequently be seen basking in direct sunlight, and in such situations, their body temperatures may be several degrees above the actual air temperature. On the other hand, during the hottest parts of the day, these animals either seek shaded areas or retreat under the water's surface where they readily "dump" excess body heat into the water. Terrestrial turtles, by contrast, avoid heat by seeking burrows or brush piles, and they may avoid the hottest parts of the day altogether and seek such refuges until the evening (or the next morning) brings cooler temperatures.

Most terrestrial turtles prefer warm but not hot temperatures

Great Blue Heron, Catron Co., New Mexico. Although quite divergent, birds are the closest living relatives to crocodilians.

A group of *Pseudemys gorzugi* basks on an exposed log in order to elevate their body temperatures before resuming foraging activities in a cool, spring-fed stream. Kinney Co., Texas.

A *Gopherus berlandieri* seeks refuge from midday heat by burrowing into loose surface debris in the shade of a large mesquite tree. Hidalgo Co., Texas.

and are typically most active in temperatures ranging from 20°
to 30°C (68°–86°F) and curtail their activity when temperatures
exceed this range. Aquatic turtles may also prefer temperatures
in a similar range, but due to the cooling effects of their aquatic
environments, rather than facing a need to cool off aquatic turtles are faced with staying warm. Most aquatic turtles and crocodilians periodically haul themselves onto logs, rocks, or banks
to bask and warm themselves in the sun. This reliance on warm
daytime temperatures and available sunlight, especially on
cool days, means that these animals are most active during the
spring, summer, and fall, while their activity is curtailed in the
winter. However, even in the winter, some individuals may be
active if temperatures are warm enough and there is enough
sunshine to allow activity. Generally speaking, at least some
turtles and crocodilians can be seen basking on all but the coldest days of a Texas winter.

Reproduction
All turtles and crocodilians lay amniotic eggs that have flexible,
leathery shells. The amniotic egg represents an important adaptation that long ago freed the ancestors of these animals (along
with reptiles, birds, and mammals) from the dependency on water for reproduction. The amniotic egg consists of an embryo
surrounded by and connected to a series of membranes. These
include the yolk, which serves as a reservoir of nutrients for the
developing embryo; the allantois, which serves to contain metabolic wastes (in particular uric acid) produced by the developing embryo; the amnion, which encloses and protects the embryo; and the chorion, which lies directly beneath the egg shell
and allows the exchange of respiratory gases between the embryo and the outside environment. The ability to store metabolic waste (toxic ammonia produced as a by-product of protein
metabolism) as insoluble, nontoxic uric acid in the amniotic
egg also preadapted some turtles to life in arid environments,
where the flushing of such wastes in a liquid form (such as the
familiar urea, produced by humans) increases the risk of dehy-
dration. Interestingly, in adult turtles, the proportion of metabolic waste produced as uric acid versus the amount produced
as urea is strongly correlated with the environments inhabited
by these animals. Desert-adapted species, such as the Texas Tor-

A *Chrysemys picta* lays two of several very large eggs in a burrow constructed by digging with its hind limbs. The soil is moistened for digging by a large amount of urination. Madison Co., Iowa.

toise (*Gopherus berlandieri*), produce more waste as uric acid than as urea, while most aquatic species, such as the Spiny Softshell (*Apalone spinifera*), produce virtually all of their waste in the liquid urea form.

Most turtles simply deposit their eggs in a nest chamber dug in the ground with their hind legs. In many species, a loose sandy or loamy soil is preferred, as these soils facilitate ease of digging the nest chamber. Some species, notably some mud and musk turtles (*Kinosternon* and *Sternotherus*), may excavate nest chambers in rotting logs. Depending upon the species, the turtle may chose a nesting site in an exposed location such that the incubating eggs may be warmed by the sun or, alternatively, in a more sheltered location so that the incubating eggs do not become overheated. Species that lay their eggs in rotting vegetation may instead rely on heat produced as the vegetation decays. In addition, aquatic species must also attempt to lay their eggs far enough above a river or stream's high water mark to ensure that the nest chamber does not become flooded, causing the developing embryos to drown. In some areas, the embankments of elevated roadways offer turtles sufficiently high ground to avoid flooding of their nest chambers, but in turn, turtles attempting to nest along these roadways run the risk of being killed by highway traffic. After egg laying, turtles abandon their nests and resume foraging activities in order to replenish body fat reserves in preparation for the next clutch of eggs. Most species of turtles in Texas deposit two or more clutches of eggs per year.

American Alligators (*Alligator mississippiensis*) construct nests composed of piles of aquatic vegetation, cattails, rushes, and leaves in which they lay their eggs. After laying the eggs in the nest, the nest is actively attended by the female, who may add or remove vegetation from the nest during the incubation period to better control incubating temperatures. During the incubation period, female alligators rarely stray far from their nests and actively guard their nests from potential predators. If an alligator nest is encountered in the field, retreat from the nesting area with caution, as a defensive mother is likely nearby!

Sex determination—whether or not an egg will produce a male or female offspring—in turtles can be controlled either genetically or by incubation temperature. In those species in which gender is under genetic control, sex is determined in much the same way as it is in humans—an offspring with two X chromosomes (XX) will be female while an offspring with an X and a Y chromosome (XY) will be male. In other species, the sex of offspring is determined by incubation temperature. In some cases, eggs incubated at cool temperatures will be males, while those incubated at warm temperatures will be females. In turtles that lay large clutches of eggs, generally speaking the eggs nearer the surface of the nest chamber incubate at warmer temperatures than those deeper underground, resulting in females hatching from eggs near the top and males hatching from eggs near the bottom. In other species, *both* low and high temperatures result in females and intermediate temperatures produce males. This is also the way sex is determined in eggs of the American Alligator and most other crocodilians.

Behavior

Animal behavior describes the various ways in which an animal interacts with the environment as well as with individuals of its own and other species. For turtles and crocodilians, these behaviors can be divided into four broad categories: thermoregulatory behaviors, which involve controlling body temperature; reproductive behaviors, which involve both attracting mates and competing with members of the same sex for the opportunity to mate; foraging behaviors, which involve the search for food; and anti-predator behaviors, which involve avoiding becoming food for other animals.

Thermoregulatory behaviors in most aquatic turtles and crocodilians revolve around two factors: controlling the animal's exposure to sunlight as a heat source and controlling the animal's exposure to water as a source of heat loss. These two factors result in the animals cycling between periods of basking to warm their bodies and periods of foraging or searching for mates underwater in which they cool off. Turtles inhabiting cooler bodies of water, such as the cold springs and streams fed by the Edwards Aquifer, may spend a much greater proportion of their time basking than turtles inhabiting lowland river floodplain swamps. On cool or cloudy days, limited sunlight may require longer basking periods than do hot, sunny days. For example, during midsummer, sightings of basking turtles may be few and far between, as most of any individual turtle's time is spent foraging beneath the water's surface, while on a cloudy day in the fall, basking turtles may be extremely numerous, as a far greater proportion of each turtle's time is spent warming out of the water.

Terrestrial species, on the other hand, must contend with controlling their exposure to sunlight as well as their contact with heated surfaces. Because terrestrial species are not able to submerge beneath the water's surface periodically, their activity patterns may be limited to cooler morning and afternoon hours, while they retreat into burrows, brush piles, or other shelters during the hottest parts of the day.

Reproductive behaviors may involve maintaining and defending a territory, competing with members of the same sex for opportunities to mate, attracting and courting a mate, avoiding the attention of unwanted suitors, engaging in physical copulatory behaviors, laying eggs, and guarding nests. In most turtles, reproductive activity occurs primarily in the spring but may also occur throughout the animal's seasonal activity period. In Texas, most turtle species may produce as many as three or four clutches of eggs during the active season. In some species, a single breeding may allow for the production of a season's worth of egg clutches.

In the American Alligator (*Alligator mississippiensis*), males actively defend a territory, which may include the home ranges of one or more females, against other males. Males do so by a variety of means, including roaring, slapping the water with their tails, and threatening with open-mouthed displays. If these postures and displays are insufficient to deter an intruder, the male may escalate his aggression to include physical combat. Such combat generally involves biting the limbs or head of the opposing male. The loser of such a territorial conflict generally is evicted from the territory. Males also use these displays to attract females and to express their willingness to mate.

Most turtle species are nonterritorial and generally search for females as they go about their daily activities in the environment. Terrestrial species may search for females by following scent trails left behind by the females, while aquatic species typically simply encounter females as they go about their day-to-day business of foraging. Nonterritoriality does not necessarily allow males of these species to avoid conflict with other males; two males may encounter a receptive female at the same time, at which point the two males will engage in first ritual and then physical conflict to win access to the female. Combat between male turtles may involve biting and clawing at one another or, particularly in terrestrial species, attempting to flip an opponent onto its back. Tortoises possess gular flanges on their plastrons that are used specifically for this purpose.

In some species, males may simply chase receptive females until the female submits and allows copulation (or until the male tires, and the unwilling female escapes his attentions). In other species, particularly the cooters (*Pseudemys*) and sliders (*Trachemys*), males possess elongated claws on their forelimbs that they use to entice a female to mate. In these species, mating occurs underwater, and males swim toward a potential mate, the direction of approach and caresses varying from species to species. If she permits his approach, he then begins to gently stroke her head, neck, and forelimbs with his elongated claws. If the female accepts his advances, she then allows copulation.

Copulation in turtles involves the male climbing onto the female's back and extending his tail under the edge of her shell in order to align their cloacae (the common openings of their reproductive, digestive, and excretory systems) and transfer sperm. Turtles have a relatively unspecialized penis by which sperm transfer. This structure is enclosed inside his cloaca and must be everted in order to inseminate the female. The male may hold on to the front rim of her carapace with his forelimbs and mouth. In terrestrial species such as box turtles (*Terrapene*) and tortoises (*Gopherus*), the male's plastron may be concave to more readily facilitate mounting the female.

Crocodilians also have a relatively unspecialized penis, similar to that found in turtles. During copulation the male must entice the female to elevate her pelvis and tail to allow the male to curl his pelvis and tail beneath her. The male may grasp the female's body with his limbs. Mating typically occurs in shallow water.

Turtles and crocodilians employ primarily two behavioral strategies of foraging: sit-and-wait and active searching; however these strategies fall at the ends of a continuum, and some species, particularly the American Alligator (*Alligator mississippiensis*), may utilize both strategies. A sit-and-wait strategy is adopted by most softshell and snapping turtles. These turtles typically feed by positioning themselves on the bottom of a body of water and waiting until their prey, typically small fish or arthropods, come into range. By rapidly opening their mouths as they lunge toward their prey, water is sucked into their gullets, "vacuuming" the prey into their mouths, where it is caught with a quick snap of their jaws. Alligator Snapping Turtles (*Macrochelys temminckii*) actually lure their prey into their jaws by employing a blood-filled, pink extension of their tongues. These giant turtles sit on the bottom of a river or stream with their mouths agape, wiggling their tongue lure until a small fish investigates it, whereupon they snap their jaws shut. Active foragers, on the other hand, move through their environment, constantly probing in and around objects in search of prey items. Most omnivorous and herbivorous species, including tortoises (*Gopherus*), box turtles (*Terrapene*), sliders (*Trachemys*), cooters (*Pseudemys*), mud turtles (*Kinosternon*), and musk turtles (*Sternotherus*), are active foragers.

Finally, turtles and crocodilians must employ behaviors that

This large adult *Pseudemys concinna* has survived a predation attempt that resulted in the loss of one of its hind legs. Panola Co., Texas. Photo by Toby J. Hibbitts.

Many aquatic turtles may be camouflaged by an extensive growth of algae on their carapace, as seen in this *Sternotherus odoratus.* Montgomery Co., Arkansas.

allow them to avoid becoming prey for other species. Adult turtles, due to their armored shell, and alligators, due to their huge size, typically face limited threat of predation. Terrestrial box turtles (*Terrapene*) are able to withdraw their vulnerable heads and limbs completely into the protection of their shells. Tortoises (*Gopherus*) are able to protect their heads with their armored forelimbs. Although large aquatic turtles cannot withdraw completely into their shells, they are capable swimmers, and few aquatic predators possess the ability to reach into the confines of their shell and attack their vulnerable limbs. Faced with selection pressures from predation by crocodilians, some aquatic turtles have highly domed shells, better to withstand the pressures of an alligator's bite. Snapping turtles (Chelydridae), mud and musk turtles (Kinosternidae), and softshell turtles (Trionychidae) may be quick to bite in self-defense, possessing sharp, powerful beaks. Many aquatic turtles may also rely on camouflage to avoid predators. Not only are some species cryptically colored, dense growth of algae may cover their carapace, helping them to blend in with their surroundings.

MAJOR WATERSHEDS IN TEXAS AND TURTLE DIVERSITY

The majority of the world's turtle species are aquatic or semi-aquatic. Many of these species are associated with river systems, particularly in arid and semi-arid portions of the country. Furthermore, numerous turtle species show a high degree of endemism—that is, they are found only in a particular area—within a specific river system. Map turtles (*Graptemys* spp.) of the southeastern United States are particularly associated with this phenomenon. In order to better understand turtle diversity in an area, it is important to have an understanding of the river systems and their characteristics in that given area.

A drainage basin is a land area that contributes water to a stream or river. Each of Texas' 11,247 streams has its own drainage basin, which includes all of the land area that feeds that stream down to its confluence with a larger stream or river. Drainage basins are divided from one another by areas of higher ground known as divides, where water that falls as precipitation on one side of a divide feeds into one drainage basin while precipitation on the other side of a divide feeds into a different drainage basin. Through the effects of erosion, rivers and streams reshape their drainage basins and in turn reshape the Earth's surface. Drainage basins may change in dynamic ways over geologic time, driven by the forces of erosion and uplifting. For example, the upper Tennessee River drainage basin was once independent of the Mississippi drainage basin, ultimately draining south into the Gulf of Mexico. Over time, erosion wore

Small, swift streams such as Boykin Creek in Jasper Co., Texas, provide limited habitat for a few species of aquatic turtles.

Numerous small rivers (many of which would be called large streams in wetter climates than Texas) serve as tributaries to larger rivers or flow directly into the Gulf of Mexico, such as the Lavaca River in Gonzales Co., Texas. Photo by John T. Williams.

Large rivers, such as the Colorado River in Colorado Co., Texas, support the largest and most diverse communities of turtles and crocodilians in Texas.

Oxbow lakes, such as Bouton Lake in Jasper Co., Texas, are habitat to many species of aquatic turtles.

down the divide between the upper and lower portions of this system, resulting in a change of course for the upper Tennessee River that joined it to the lower Tennessee River and connected it as part of the Mississippi River drainage. River drainage basins vary greatly, and each is unique, reflecting climate, geology, topography, and vegetation.

Coastal marshes, such as this site in Matagorda Co., Texas, support dense populations of turtles that prefer stagnant waters, such as Eastern Mud Turtles (*Kinosternon subrubrum*) and Pond Sliders (*Trachemys scripta*). As waters become more brackish, these species are replaced by Texas' only estuarine-dwelling species, the Diamondback Terrapin (*Malaclemys terrapin*).

There are 128,720 km (80,000 mi.) of rivers and streams in Texas draining a land area of 682,599 km² (263,513 mi.²). As of this publication, 212 reservoirs have been constructed on Texas rivers and streams. The river systems in Texas can be divided into approximately 12 river drainages, several of which are minor rivers that possess turtle faunas similar to those of nearby major rivers. Most have their headwaters in Texas, with the exceptions being the Mississippi and Rio Grande drainages, and flow southeastward to the Gulf of Mexico, supplying nutrients and water necessary for maintaining diverse ecosystems, wildlife populations, agricultural production, and human populations.

In general, turtle diversity in a watershed increases as stream flow in that river system increases. The upper reaches of most watersheds are lacking in turtle diversity, consisting of only a few generalist species, while diversity increases as one moves toward the coastal plain and the Gulf of Mexico. Diversity also increases in a system as a function of overall rainfall, with greater turtle diversity in moist, eastern portions of the state and less diversity in the arid west. However, the isolation of river systems in the drier portions of the state has led to speciation in several turtle groups (notably *Graptemys*, *Pseudemys*, and *Trachemys*), resulting in the evolution of several species endemic to western Texas rivers. See appendix C for a quick reference table outlining the turtle species present in each river system.

For the purposes of this volume, we have identified eight major river drainages in the state, ranging from the Mississippi River watershed, which drains most of central North America, to the Guadalupe River drainage, which drains a relatively small portion of Central Texas. Minor river systems, such as the San Jacinto and Lavaca rivers along the Texas coast, are briefly discussed along with their neighboring major river drainages. For the purposes of this volume, a major river drainage is one that drains directly into the Gulf of Mexico and is greater than 193 km (120 mi.) in length.

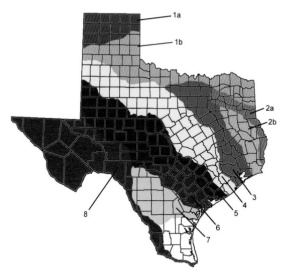

Major watersheds of Texas: 1a. Canadian River; 1b. Red River; 2a. Sabine River; 2b. Neches River; 3. Trinity River. 4. Brazos River; 5. Colorado River; 6. Guadalupe River; 7. Nueces River; and 8. Rio Grande. The region in South Texas depicted in white is drained by scattered small streams that flow directly into Corpus Christi Bay and the Laguna Madre.

Mississippi Watershed

The watershed of the Mississippi River is the fourth largest in the world, encompassing approximately 40% of the continental United States and draining 3.1 million square kilometers (1.2 million square miles). The watershed extends from the Appalachian Mountains in the east to the Rocky Mountains in the west and includes all or parts of 31 states and 2 Canadian provinces. From its headwaters in Lake Itasca, Minnesota, to its mouth south of New Orleans, Louisiana, the mainstem of the river is approximately 3781 km (2350 mi.) long. The only turtle species that is strictly endemic to the Mississippi drainage is the Ouachita Map Turtle (*Graptemys ouachitensis*). In addition, several species are broadly endemic to the region composed of the Mississippi River and neighboring smaller rivers along the Gulf Coast, including the Alligator Snapping Turtle (*Macrochelys temminckii*), the False Map Turtle (*Graptemys pseudogeographica*), the Painted Turtle (*Chrysemys picta*), the Razor-backed Musk Turtle (*Sternotherus carinatus*), and the Smooth Softshell (*Apalone spinifera*).

Major tributaries of the Mississippi include the Missouri River, with headwaters in western Montana; the Ohio River, with headwaters in Pennsylvania and New York; and the Arkansas River, with headwaters in central Colorado. Texas contains portions of two major tributaries of the Mississippi—the Canadian and Red rivers.

CANADIAN RIVER The Canadian River runs from west to east across the Texas panhandle in Oldham, Potter, Moore, Hutchinson, Roberts, and Hemphill counties. Its length through Texas is 343 km (213 mi.), and its watershed drains 33,320 km^2 (12,865 mi.^{2}), including all or parts of 15 of the northernmost counties in the state. The headwaters of the Canadian River are located at Raton Pass, New Mexico. Conchos Lake Dam, in northeastern New Mexico, stops most of the flow of the Canadian River through Texas. Lake Meredith, in Potter, Moore, and Hutchinson counties, is the only reservoir constructed on the Canadian River in Texas.

No turtle species is endemic to Texas portions of the Canadian River, and in Texas the turtle fauna associated with this system is not very diverse. It primarily consists of widespread generalist species including the Snapping Turtle (*Chelydra ser-*

The Canadian River, shown here below Lake Meredith in Hutchinson Co., Texas, is often an intermittently flowing, shallow, sandy stream along its length in the Texas Panhandle. Photo by Michael A. Smith.

pentina), the River Cooter (*Pseudemys concinna*), the Pond Slider (*Trachemys scripta*), the Yellow Mud Turtle (*Kinosternon flavescens*), the Smooth Softshell (*Apalone mutica*), and the Spiny Softshell (*Apalone spinifera*).

RED RIVER The Red River is a tributary of the Mississippi and Atchafalaya river complex, draining a land area that includes parts of Texas, Oklahoma, Arkansas, and Louisiana. Its headwaters are in Palo Duro Canyon in Randall County, Texas, and it is 2188 km (1360 mi.) long, with 2076 km (1290 mi.) of that length in Texas, forming the border with Oklahoma for much of that distance. The Red River drainage in Texas encompasses 62,929 km² (24,297 mi.²) and includes all or parts of 50 Texas counties. Throughout its length in Texas, the Red River runs from west to east, turning south toward the Gulf of Mexico and its confluence with the Atchafalaya–Mississippi a few miles to the east of Texarkana in southeastern Arkansas. Its name is derived both from reddish sediments suspended in the stream's flow and reddish sandbars deposited along its banks for much of its length. These sediments originate from the fine red sands and clays present in much of the upper portions of the watershed.

Tributaries of the Red River in Texas include the Prairie

Dog Town Fork, the North Fork, the Salt Fork, the Pease River, the Wichita River, the Sulphur River, and Cypress Creek. Lake Texoma is the largest reservoir in the system. Other reservoirs include Lake Kemp, Lake Wichita, Lake Arrowhead, Cooper Lake, Cypress Springs Lake, Lake Bob Sandlin, Lake Monticello, Wright Patman Lake, Lake O'Pines, and Caddo Lake.

Turtle diversity in the Red River increases from west to east with the greatest diversity of species in the northeastern portion of the state. Species present in the Red River system include the Snapping Turtle (*Chelydra serpentina*), the Alligator Snapping Turtle (*Macrochelys temminckii*), the Ouachita Map Turtle (*Graptemys ouachitensis*), the False Map Turtle (*Graptemys pseudogeographica*), the River Cooter (*Pseudemys concinna*), the Painted Turtle (*Chrysemys picta*), the Chicken Turtle (*Deirochelys reticularia*), the Pond Slider (*Trachemys scripta*), the Yellow Mud Turtle (*Kinosternon flavescens*), the Eastern Mud Turtle (*Kinosternon subrubrum*), the Razor-backed Musk Turtle (*Sternotherus carinatus*), the Stinkpot (*Sternotherus odoratus*), the Smooth Softshell (*Apalone mutica*), and the Spiny Softshell (*Apalone spinifera*). The American Alligator (*Alligator mississippiensis*) occurs in the lower portions of the Red River and its tributaries.

The Red River, shown here in Montague Co., Texas, near Ringgold, owes its name to its red sandy banks, which also color its stream flow. Photo by Bryan Box.

Upon reaching the northeast corner of the state, the flow of the Red River swells to an impressive volume, Bowie Co., Texas.

Caddo Lake, spanning the Texas-Louisiana state line in Marion and Harrison counties, is Texas' largest natural lake and supports highly productive cypress swamps similar to those seen farther to the southeast in the Mississippi River Delta of Louisiana.

Sabine and Neches Watersheds

The Sabine and Neches rivers make up two related watersheds near the Louisiana border in deep East Texas. Both drain into Sabine Lake at Port Arthur, and they share most of the same turtle species (as well as fish and other fauna). Like most Texas rivers, they trend from northwest to southeast as they flow toward the Gulf of Mexico. The Sabine and Neches watersheds are home to a single endemic turtle species, the Sabine Map Turtle (*Graptemys sabinensis*). Other species present in both the Sabine and Neches watersheds include the Snapping Turtle (*Chelydra serpentina*), the Alligator Snapping Turtle (*Macrochelys temminckii*), the False Map Turtle (*Graptemys pseudogeographica*), the River Cooter (*Pseudemys concinna*), the Chicken Turtle (*Deirochelys reticularia*), the Pond Slider (*Trachemys scripta*), the Yellow Mud Turtle (*Kinosternon flavescens*), the Eastern Mud Turtle (*Kinosternon subrubrum*), the Razor-backed Musk Turtle (*Sternotherus carinatus*), the Stinkpot (*Sternotherus odoratus*), the Smooth Softshell (*Apalone mutica*), and the Spiny Softshell (*Apalone spinifera*). The American Alligator (*Alligator mississippiensis*) occurs throughout both drainages.

SABINE RIVER The headwaters of the Sabine River are in Hunt County northeast of Dallas. From its headwaters, it con-

The Sabine River drains much of the Pineywoods of extreme East Texas as well as parts of adjacent Louisiana. It possesses a substantial stream flow, even as far north as Carthage in Panola Co., Texas.

tinues in a southeasterly direction to the Louisiana border where it turns southward on its journey to the Gulf of Mexico. From Shelby County southward, it makes up the border between Texas and Louisiana. The river is 579 km (360 mi.) long and drains 19,606 km² (7570 mi.²) of Texas, including all or parts of 20 Texas counties. The largest reservoir in the state of Texas, Toledo Bend Reservoir, an impoundment of 75,330 ha (186,000 acres), extends 105 km (65 mi.) from Panola County to Newton County. For much of its length, the Sabine River is a sandy-bottomed stream, and the lower portions were frequently subject to substantial flooding. In part, Toledo Bend Reservoir was constructed to control these floods. Other reservoirs in the system include Lake Tawakoni and Lake Fork.

In addition to the species listed above, the Painted Turtle (*Chrysemys picta*) is present in parts of the upper portion of the Sabine watershed, primarily in the upper reaches of Toledo Bend Reservoir.

NECHES RIVER The Neches River, along with its tributary the Angelina River, drains 25,734 km² (9937 mi.²) consisting of all or parts of 20 Texas counties. The entire 669 km (416 mi.) length of the river is contained in Texas, from its headwaters in Van Zandt County south to Sabine Lake. Reservoirs on the system include

The Neches River, seen here in Tyler Co., Texas, runs throughout the Pineywoods of deep East Texas. Photo by John T. Williams.

Steinhagen Reservoir (seen here at Martin Dies Jr. State Park in Sabine Co., Texas) inundates the confluence of the Neches River and its largest tributary, the Angelina River.

The upper reaches of the Angelina River may be shallow and offer abundant snags for basking turtles. Nacogdoches County, Texas. Photo by John T. Williams.

Sam Rayburn Reservoir (the second largest reservoir in Texas), Lake Palestine, and B. A. Steinhagen Reservoir. The lower portions of the Neches River pass through the Big Thicket National Preserve, an important ecosphere preserve that protects a variety of ecosystems ranging from riparian floodplain to remnant longleaf pine savannahs and flatwoods pitcher plant bogs.

Trinity Watershed

The Trinity River consists of four major forks: the Clear Fork, West Fork, Elm Fork, and East Fork. The headwaters are, respectively, in Parker, Archer, Montague, and Grayson counties. The Trinity is 888 km (552 mi.) long and drains a land area of 46,395 km^2 (17,913 mi.^{2}) covering all or parts of 36 Texas counties. Much of the land area drained by the Trinity River consists of the Dallas–Fort Worth metroplex and land devoted to extensive agricultural use; therefore the Trinity is generally regarded as the most polluted river in Texas. Its forks merge in the Dallas–Fort Worth metro area, after which the river flows southeastward to Trinity Bay on the east side of Houston. Numerous dams impound reservoirs on the Trinity or its tributaries, including Lake Livingston, Cedar Creek Lake, Richland-Chambers Res-

The upper reaches of the Trinity River occur in a primarily urban landscape and have been channelized in an effort to control flooding, as can be seen at this site in Tarrant Co., Texas. Photo by Mallory Fontenot.

Near its confluence with the Gulf of Mexico, the Trinity is a large and impressive river, Liberty Co., Texas. Photo by John T. Williams.

ervoir, Lake Lewisville, Eagle Mountain Lake, Lake Bridgeport, Benbrook Lake, Lave Lavon, and Lake Ray Hubbard.

The San Jacinto River empties into Trinity Bay a few miles to the west of the mouth of the Trinity and shares much of the same flora and fauna with its larger sister. The San Jacinto is 138 km (85 mi.) long and drains a land area of 10,194 km² (3936 mi.²) in Walker, Grimes, Waller, Harris, San Jacinto, and Liberty counties. Lakes on the San Jacinto River include Lake Conroe and Lake Houston.

Turtles inhabiting the Trinity and San Jacinto River watersheds include the Snapping Turtle (*Chelydra serpentina*), the Alligator Snapping Turtle (*Macrochelys temminckii*), the False Map Turtle (*Graptemys pseudogeographica*), the River Cooter (*Pseudemys concinna*), the Chicken Turtle (*Deirochelys reticularia*), the Pond Slider (*Trachemys scripta*), the Yellow Mud Turtle (*Kinosternon flavescens*), the Eastern Mud Turtle (*Kinosternon subrubrum*), the Razor-backed Musk Turtle (*Sternotherus carinatus*), the Stinkpot (*Sternotherus odoratus*), the Smooth Softshell (*Apalone mutica*), and the Spiny Softshell (*Apalone spinifera*). The American Alligator (*Alligator mississippiensis*) occurs in the Trinity River from the vicinity of Dallas southward to the coast.

Brazos Watershed

The Brazos River is often referenced as the longest river contained entirely in Texas. Its headwaters are generally considered to be springs present at the base of the caprock near Lubbock; however, its watershed also includes some normally dry draws and washes that drain parts of eastern New Mexico during periods of heavy rainfall. The Brazos River is 1368 km (850 mi.) long and drains 108,780 km^2 (42,000 mi.^{2}) of Texas consisting of all or parts of 70 Texas counties. The Brazos empties into the Gulf of Mexico at Freeport southwest of Houston. Its tributaries include the Clear Fork, Mountain Fork, Middle Fork, Leon, Paluxy, Little Brazos, and Navasota rivers. The nearby San Bernard River empties into the Gulf of Mexico a few miles to the west and, faunally, can be classified as part of this system. Nineteen reservoirs have been constructed on the Brazos and its tributaries, including Possum Kingdom Lake, Lake Whitney, Lake Waco, and Belton Lake.

Turtles present in the Brazos drainage include the Snapping Turtle (*Chelydra serpentina*), the False Map Turtle (*Graptemys pseudogeographica*), the Texas River Cooter (*Pseudemys texana*), the Chicken Turtle (*Deirochelys reticularia*), the Pond Slider (*Trachemys scripta*), the Yellow Mud Turtle (*Kinosternon fla-*

The upper reaches of the Brazos River are interspersed with areas of rocky riffles, such as this site in Somervell Co., Texas.

The lower Brazos is a large river that carries an abundant sediment flow. Brazos Co., Texas.

vescens), the Eastern Mud Turtle (*Kinosternon subrubrum*), the Razor-backed Musk Turtle (*Sternotherus carinatus*), the Stinkpot (*Sternotherus odoratus*), the Smooth Softshell (*Apalone mutica*), and the Spiny Softshell (*Apalone spinifera*). Noticeable phenotypic differences exist between populations of False Map Turtles present in the lower portion of the Brazos and those occurring in the Clear Fork of the Brazos. The American Alligator (*Alligator mississippiensis*) occurs in the Brazos River from the vicinity of Waco south to the coast.

Colorado Watershed

The Colorado River drains much of the Edwards Plateau of Central Texas. Its headwaters are generally considered to arise from springs just below the caprock in Borden County; during periods of heavy rainfall, runoff may flow into the Colorado along washes and draws extending nearly to the New Mexico border. The Colorado River is 1391 km (865 mi.) long, drains a land area of 109,604 km² (42,318 mi.²) consisting of all or parts of 56 Texas counties, and empties into the Gulf of Mexico just to the east of Matagorda Bay. Its major tributaries include the Concho, San Saba, Llano, and Pedernales rivers, as well as Pecan Bayou, the only major tributary on the east side of the main river. The

Lavaca River empties into Matagorda Bay a few miles west of the Colorado and shares many of the same plant and animal species. Reservoirs on the Colorado system include Lake Buchanan, Lake Travis, Lake LBJ, Marble Falls Lake, Lady Bird Lake, O. H. Ivie Reservoir, Twin Buttes Reservoir, O. C. Fisher Lake, and E. V. Spence Reservoir.

A single species, the Texas Map Turtle (*Graptemys versa*), is endemic to the Colorado River system. Other species that occur in the Colorado River system include the Snapping Turtle (*Chelydra serpentina*), the Texas River Cooter (*Pseudemys texana*), the Chicken Turtle (*Deirochelys reticularia*), the Pond Slider (*Trachemys scripta*), the Yellow Mud Turtle (*Kinosternon flavescens*), the Eastern Mud Turtle (*Kinosternon subrubrum*), the Stinkpot (*Sternotherus odoratus*), the Smooth Softshell (*Apalone mutica*), and the Spiny Softshell (*Apalone spinifera*). The

Sections of riffles become widely separated as the Colorado River flows toward the edge of the Balcones Escarpment, such as this site in San Saba Co., Texas.

Near flood stage after heavy spring or summer rains, the Colorado supports an impressive stream flow and dense load of reddish sediment, which gives the river its name.

The Llano River is one of the Colorado River's most important tributaries. It is a clear-water stream with much of its flow derived from springs of the Edwards Plateau. Kimble Co., Texas.

The Llano River photographed in the city of Llano, Llano Co., Texas.

American Alligator (*Alligator mississippiensis*) occurs in the Colorado River from Austin to the coast.

Guadalupe Watershed

The Guadalupe River and its associated watershed are among the smallest of the major river systems in Texas. The river arises from springs in Kerr and Bandera counties and travels 658 km (409 mi.) east-southeast into the Gulf of Mexico at San Antonio Bay. Its tributaries include the San Antonio, Medina, Blanco, Comal, and San Marcos rivers. Combined, these drain a land area of 17,837 km² (6887 mi.²) including all or parts of 19 Texas counties. Its course is supplied by numerous major springs along the Balcones Escarpment, including Comal Springs, the largest spring in the state. Major reservoirs in the system include Medina and Canyon lakes; in addition, numerous small dams are present throughout the system that affect stream flow and turtle populations.

The Guadalupe River is home to a single species of endemic turtle, the Cagle's Map Turtle (*Graptemys caglei*), which is confined primarily to portions of the Guadalupe and Blanco rivers with ample stream flow near areas of rapids and riffles. Other species present include the Snapping Turtle (*Chelydra serpentina*), the Texas River Cooter (*Pseudemys texana*), the Chicken

The upper portions of the Guadalupe River in Kerr Co. are widely considered to be among the most beautiful stretches of river in Texas. Photos by Tony Galluci.

Turtle (*Deirochelys reticularia*), the Pond Slider (*Trachemys scripta*), the Yellow Mud Turtle (*Kinosternon flavescens*), the Eastern Mud Turtle (*Kinosternon subrubrum*), the Stinkpot (*Sternotherus odoratus*), and the Spiny Softshell (*Apalone spinifera*). In addition, the Florida Red-bellied Cooter (*Pseudemys nelsoni*) has been introduced into Spring Lake at the headwaters of the San Marcos River. The American Alligator (*Alliga-*

On the coastal plain, the Guadalupe loses some of its scenic beauty, such as can be seen at this site in Victoria Co., Texas, but remains home to the threatened Cagle's Map Turtle (*Graptemys caglei*). Photo by John T. Williams.

tor mississippiensis) occurs sparingly in this system from New Braunfels to the coast.

Nueces River

The Nueces River and its tributaries—the Frio, Sabinal, and Atascosa—drain the southern flanks of the Balcones Escarpment and empty into Corpus Christi Bay. The Nueces is 507 km (315 mi.) long, and the basin drains 43,926 km² (16,960 mi.²) including all or parts of 21 Texas counties. The headwaters of the Nueces arise from springs in Edwards and Real counties. Surface flow in the Nueces and Frio rivers, particularly as they traverse the faulted Balcones Escarpment, is discontinuous and underground in most years, particularly during times of drought. Few large reservoirs have been impounded on the rivers of this system, with Choke Canyon Reservoir and Lake Corpus Christi being the only major ones present.

The turtle fauna in this drainage is discontinuous but includes the Pond Slider (*Trachemys scripta*), the Yellow Mud Turtle (*Kinosternon flavescens*), the Stinkpot (*Sternotherus odoratus*), and the Spiny Softshell (*Apalone spinifera*). In addition, the Snapping Turtle (*Chelydra serpentina*) and the Texas River

The headwaters of the Nueces in Edwards and Real counties are represented by intermittently flowing sections of spring-fed streams; turtle diversity is fairly low in these sites.

The rocky, spring-fed upper reaches of the Nueces River in Real and Edwards counties are habitat to a few species of turtles, primarily *Trachemys scripta*, *Sternotherus odoratus*, and *Apalone spinifera*.

Following spring and summer rains, the shallow flow of the Nueces River can be transformed into a raging torrent. Real Co., Texas.

Throughout much of its length in South Texas, the Nueces River, seen here at flood stage, traverses dense thornscrub habitats. Due to its intermittent and slow-moving nature, it supports primarily pond species such as the Pond Slider (*Trachemys scripta*). Dimmitt Co., Texas.

The Frio River is fed at its headwaters by several large springs, and the river emerges from these springs in an impressive flow, as can be seen at this site in Real Co., Texas. Photo by Tony Galluci.

Cooter (*Pseudemys texana*) are present in the upper reaches of the Frio and Sabinal rivers, and the Eastern Mud Turtle (*Kinosternon subrubrum*) is present in the lower floodplains near the Gulf of Mexico. The American Alligator (*Alligator mississippiensis*) occurs as far up the Nueces as Carrizo Springs and in the Frio as far inland as the vicinity of Pearsall.

Rio Grande Watershed

The Rio Grande watershed drains much of the landscape in the southwestern United States as well as significant portions of northern Mexico. Tributaries to the Rio Grande include the Pecos and Devils rivers in the United States and the Rio Conchos, Rio Salado, and Rio San Juan in Mexico. Its drainage basin encompasses 471,898 km² (182,200 mi.²) in the United States and Mexico. In Texas, the Rio Grande drainage includes 127,912 km² (49,387 mi.²) and all or parts of 32 Texas counties.

Two species of turtle are endemic to the Rio Grande drainage. The Rio Grande Cooter (*Pseudemys gorzugi*) occurs in the Rio Grande downstream of Brewster County, in the Pecos River with a hiatus in distribution from Red Bluff Reservoir to Terrell County, and in the Devils River. The Mexican Plateau Slider (*Trachemys gaigeae*) occurs in the Rio Grande from Ter-

The crystal clear waters of the upper Frio River, part of the Nueces River drainage, are home to *Pseudemys texana*, *Trachemys scripta*, *Sternotherus odoratus*, and *Apalone spinifera*. Uvalde Co., Texas.

rell County to Hudspeth County, with a disjunct population in central New Mexico. While not endemic to the Rio Grande, a third species that ranges widely in Mexico, the Rough-footed Mud Turtle (*Kinosternon hirtipes*), occurs in the United States only in the Rio Grande drainage, reaching the northernmost part of its distribution at Alamito Creek, a small tributary of the Rio Grande in the Trans Pecos. Other species present in the

The Rio Grande provides an oasis of life-bringing water to an otherwise parched desert landscape. Presidio Co., Texas.

The Rio Grande carves several impressive canyons in the Big Bend region of Texas, including Santa Elena Canyon in Brewster Co., Texas. These sites are home to *Trachemys gaigeae* and *Apalone spinifera*.

Rio Grande drainage include the Snapping Turtle (*Chelydra serpentina*), the Painted Turtle (*Chrysemys picta*), the Pond Slider (*Trachemys scripta*), the Yellow Mud Turtle (*Kinosternon flavescens*), and the Spiny Softshell (*Apalone spinifera*). The American Alligator (*Alligator mississippiensis*) occurs in coastal

The Lower Canyons of the Rio Grande, in Terrell Co., Texas, are habitat for *Pseudemys gorzugi, Trachemys scripta,* and *Apalone spinifera.*

In the Lower Rio Grande Valley in Hidalgo Co., Texas, the Rio Grande is a large, slow-moving river delivering a large volume of water that is used to irrigate agricultural lands of the region.

marshes near the mouth of the Rio Grande and in the river itself below Falcon Reservoir.

RIO GRANDE The headwaters of the Rio Grande are in the San Juan Mountains of Colorado, and the river traverses 3057 km

43

(1900 mi.) before it reaches the Gulf of Mexico near Brownsville. From just north of El Paso to its mouth, it forms the border between Mexico and the United States. Except in wet years, its stream flow ends near the end of the El Paso Valley and starts again at the Rio Conchos. Major reservoirs on the Rio Grande include Elephant Butte Reservoir in New Mexico and Lake Amistad and Falcon Lake along the border between Texas and Mexico.

PECOS RIVER The largest tributary of the Rio Grande in the United States is the Pecos River. From its headwaters in the Sangre de Cristo Mountains of New Mexico to its confluence with the Rio Grande it extends for 1533 km (953 mi.) and drains a land area of 113,960 km^2 (44,000 mi.^{2}) in New Mexico and Texas. The only reservoir on the Pecos in Texas is Red Bluff Reservoir, extending from Reeves and Loving counties in Texas north into New Mexico. In addition, at its maximum water level, Lake Amistad inundates the lower Pecos River at its confluence with the Rio Grande.

Much of the Pecos River between Red Bluff Reservoir and Terrell County is noted for its high salt content. This is due to reduced stream flow, saline water intrusions, and high rates of evaporation in this arid region. Many of the turtles characteris-

Where the Pecos River flows across the western edge of the Permian Basin it is a stagnant, salty stream with reduced stream flow and is inhabited by very few turtles. Pecos Co., Texas.

The spring-fed lower reaches of the Pecos River in Val Verde Co., Texas, are home to *Pseudemys gorzugi*, *Trachemys scripta*, and *Apalone spinifera*.

Near its confluence with the Rio Grande in Val Verde Co., Texas, the Pecos River has carved a deep and impressive canyon in the landscape. This portion of the river is typically inundated by the waters of Amistad Reservoir.

tic of the Rio Grande River system are absent from this stretch of the Pecos, notably the Rio Grande Cooter (*Pseudemys gorzugi*). Beginning in Terrell County, the Pecos is replenished by numerous springs associated with the western portion of the Edwards Plateau.

DEVILS RIVER The Devils River is considered to be Texas' cleanest river. Its headwaters are in Sutton County near Sonora, and its channel runs southward for 151 km (94 mi.) to its confluence with the Rio Grande near Del Rio. Much of the upper half of the Devils River is dry, with most of the stream flow under-

Texas' largest waterfall by volume, Dolan Falls, is found in a remote canyon of the upper Devils River in Val Verde Co.

The lower canyons of the Devils River have been inundated by the creation of Amistad Reservoir. Water levels here in this parched landscape are rarely maintained near capacity.

San Felipe Creek in Val Verde Co. exemplifies the beautiful nature of spring-fed streams that appear as oases in the desert landscape of west Texas.

ground. The lower portion of the Devils River is fed by numerous springs associated with the western edge of the Edwards Plateau. For much of its lower portion, the river is fairly calm with long, deep, clear pools with ample aquatic vegetation interspersed with infrequent whitewater rapids. Texas' largest waterfall by volume, Dolan Falls, is on the lower Devils River. The Devils River runs through picturesque canyons throughout its length. Unfortunately, some of the most spectacular scenic areas on the river were flooded when the Rio Grande was dammed to create Lake Amistad.

The Devils River is noted for its healthy populations of Rio Grande Cooters (*Pseudemys gorzugi*). Other turtles present in the Devils River include the Yellow Mud Turtle (*Kinosternon flavescens*), the Pond Slider (*Trachemys scripta*), and the Spiny Softshell (*Apalone spinifera*).

CONSERVATION
Habitat Loss and Fragmentation
Habitat loss encompasses a range of habitat-altering activities. Most people tend to think first of wholesale alteration of entire ecosystems when thinking of habitat loss—activities such as strip-mining, clear-cutting of a forest, plowing range land in order to convert it to agricultural uses, or bulldozing and level-

ing the landscape to clear land for a subdivision or other building project. However, many forms of habitat loss are much more subtle. An example of this less obvious type of habitat loss would be the replacement of native range grasses with grasses used in "improved pastures," such as Coastal Bermuda, King Ranch Bluestem, or Buffelgrass. However, the most widespread cause of habitat alteration to terrestrial environments in Texas results from suppression of natural fire cycles. In aquatic systems, the single greatest form of habitat alteration in Texas has been the impoundment of rivers to create reservoirs and the consequent changes to stream flow downstream of their dams.

Habitat loss or alteration affects species because they rely on their environments to provide them with conditions suitable to meet their physical needs. While some species may find a wide range of environmental conditions to be suitable and can therefore tolerate a great deal of alteration to their habitats, others may be highly specialized and require very specific conditions to be present to survive. In such instances, very minor (to a human observer!) environmental changes may result in local or widespread extirpation of that species from the landscape.

The conversion of land to agriculture has occurred widely throughout Texas, particularly in prairie situations such as the Coastal Prairies and Marshes, Post Oak Savanna, Blackland Prairies, Rolling Plains, and High Plains. Removal of these natural prairies has reduced or eliminated significant amounts of habitat for terrestrial turtle species. Further, runoff associated with agriculture has altered aquatic ecosystems both through the introduction of chemical pollutants, including fertilizers, herbicides, and pesticides, as well as by increasing the amounts of sediment suspended in Texas rivers. For example, the Trinity River drains a landscape almost entirely converted to agricultural uses and is considered to be one of the most polluted rivers in the state. Sadly and ironically, when settlers first arrived in the region this river was named Trinity at least partially in reference to the purity of its waters.

Another significant alteration to Texas' native habitats occurred when mature hardwood and pine forests of the eastern third of the state were cut for both timber and conversion to pasture lands. While at first glance it may seem that significant stands of these forests still exist, closer examination reveals that this landscape has been dramatically altered from its natural condition. Virtually all of Texas' forested lands consist of second- or third-growth stands of trees, many of which are less than 30 years old. The understories of such forests are much denser, with more shrubby vegetation than is found in a mature forest. Furthermore, many of these "forests" are in actuality little more than agricultural fields devoted to the production of a single crop—in this case, pine plantations grown for the production of wood pulp destined for paper mills. Finally, the active suppression of fires in these forests has also dramatically changed their characteristics. Much of the heart of the southeastern Texas pinelands once consisted of mature stands of Longleaf and Loblolly pines, with trees widely spaced from one another, very little understory of oaks and brush, and the forest floor carpeted with grasses. In fact, in many ways these forests could have been characterized as grassland. These conditions were naturally maintained by frequent periodic summer wildfires that burned the litter of pine needles and summer-dried grasses without damaging the mature or growing young pines and also largely prevented the growth of hardwood trees. While the suppression of wildfires remains a necessity in a landscape with human habitations scattered throughout the forest, fire suppression has negative consequences for humans as well—in a forest where significant underbrush and fuel has been allowed to accumulate, those fires that do occur are often quite catastrophic—as, for example, the Bastrop-area fires of 2011.

The suppression of natural wildfires, in fact, can be implicated in dramatic changes in habitats throughout the state. Most grassland and savanna habitats are kept free of brush by fires. At one time, the Post Oak Savannas that occurred along the Interstate 45 corridor between the Pineywoods of deep East Texas and the Blackland Prairies of Central Texas were characterized by widely spaced islands of oaks in a sea of grass. Much of the Edwards Plateau also showed similar characteristics. Today both regions show very dense forests of small oaks with a great deal of brushy undergrowth. In the Post Oak Savannas this undergrowth is predominately shrubby growth such as Yaupon Holly, while on the Edwards Plateau dense stands of Ashe Juniper choke out the grass. South of San Antonio, the landscape is often referred to as South Texas Brush Country. Yet this brushy condition so familiar to South Texas deer hunters has existed for only the past 100 years or so and is a direct result of fire suppression coupled with overgrazing. Once this landscape supported extensive stands of native grasses, with much of the brushy vegetation confined to the immediate vicinity of watercourses. These changes in habitat beginning in the late 1800s have likely had negative impacts on all three of Texas' native terrestrial turtles, as they have certainly resulted in changes to their natural food supplies.

The impoundment of many Texas rivers to create reservoirs has affected turtle and crocodilian populations in both negative and positive ways. First, damming of these rivers flooded large areas of habitat supporting terrestrial turtle species. Second, the lakes create habitat for many aquatic species, including those adapted to shallow water. Only those species of aquatic turtle that prefer shallow, flowing water (such as the Cagle's Map Turtle, *Graptemys caglei*) seem not to thrive in lakes. And third, the resulting changes in stream flow affect all aquatic ecosystems downstream of the dam, often reducing turtle populations. For example, the Colorado River below E. V. Spence Reservoir in Coke County formerly had a robust stream flow and healthy populations of Texas Map Turtles (*Graptemys versa*) but with the stream flow reduced by the dam, this section of river is often dry or with very low flow, and map turtles are now uncommon in this section of the river.

Finally, habitat fragmentation presents a special problem for many animal species, particularly those with large home ranges. As parcels of habitat become increasingly fragmented by road development, wild animals increasingly are at risk of road mortality as they attempt to cross busy highways. Long-lived species with high hatchling mortality rates are particularly impacted by this problem. Box turtles (*Terrapene* spp.) have home ranges often in excess of 2.6 km^2 (1 mi.^{2}), are long-lived as adults, and have a high hatchling mortality (approaching 99%). Habitat fragmentation and road development cause mortality in adults far in excess of the natural levels of mortality from predation, resulting in loss of adults that are not replaced by recruitment from new generations of turtles. Furthermore, habitat fragmentation may enable predator populations, such as those of raccoons and coyotes, to increase, resulting in increased predation pressures on turtles. Population densities of box turtles have been demon-

The challenge of crossing busy highways is one that slow-moving, armored turtles are ill equipped to handle. *Chelydra serpentina*, Trigg Co., Kentucky.

Many turtles are killed each year on roadways, such as this *Terrapene ornata* from Brewster Co., Texas.

strated to be far higher in roadless areas than in those bisected by even small, unpaved rural roadways. Small parcels of land with seemingly suitable habitat, particularly those bounded on all sides by roadways, may have smaller than normal populations of box turtles, or they may be absent altogether.

Pollution

Much like mammals, turtles and crocodilians, with their mostly impermeable skins, are relatively tolerant of environmental pollutants that are encountered directly. Turtles and crocodilians may be susceptible to pollutants such as pesticides, which may be present on or in the tissues of their prey, by directly ingesting prey items that have been poisoned by pesticides. Continued pesticide application may result in the reduction or elimination of prey species that make up a turtle or crocodilian's food supply. Consequently, in rural areas, turtle and crocodilian population density and species diversity are typically highest in wild or ranch lands and lowest in pesticide-intensive agricultural areas (although it must be noted that habitat structure and diversity are also higher in wild and ranch lands, thus promoting diversity and supporting higher population densities). In aquatic settings, agricultural runoff may affect aquatic vegetation in a variety of ways. Fertilizers may cause algal blooms that deplete water oxygen levels and kill aquatic plants upon which some turtles feed. In addition, herbicides that kill native plants may also be present in runoff. In most cases, those natural bodies of water that are not subject to agricultural and urban runoff, with their fertilizers, herbicides, and pesticides, support diverse natural vegetation and healthy turtle populations.

Climate Change

Climatic change is a real, readily observable phenomenon that has been globally documented. However, its effects on turtle and crocodilian populations remain unclear, with relatively few studies having been funded to explore the effects of these changes. The few published studies are quite recent, with data typically spanning less than a decade, while climate change is a long-term phenomenon best evaluated over multiple decades of observations. The general consensus is that the effects of changing climates on animal populations are complex and may be positive for some species yet negative for others. Turtle and crocodilian species reach their greatest diversity in tropical and moist temperate regions, so increasing regional or global temperatures and resulting droughts of many areas may result in the loss of habitat and decreases in the geographic ranges and populations of some species. Further, those species associated with grasslands may see their ranges contract and their populations decline as these habitats are increasingly converted to more desert-like conditions. Along with hunting by Paleolithic peoples, this desertification is thought to be part of the reason that the Bolson Tortoise (*Gopherus flavomarginatus*) of the Chihuahuan Desert became extinct in the American Southwest. Fossil evidence indicates that it was present until at least the mid-Holocene epoch, but it is now restricted to a desert-grassland drainage known as the Bolsón de Mapimi in northern Mexico.

While the above description may paint a general picture of the result of changing climates on turtle and crocodilian populations, the situation may be more complex. For example, some species of turtles and crocodilians may synchronize their reproductive cycles in such a way that the emergence of their off-spring coincides with the arrival of late-summer rainfall, which in turn results in the proliferation of plant growth and of small invertebrates that make up the primary prey of neonates. In some cases, this synchronization may be genetically determined and may not be triggered by environmental cues (or may be triggered by invariant environmental cues such as day length). In such cases, changes to seasonal rainfall patterns resulting from climate change may de-synchronize the animal's reproductive cycles with rainfall and therefore result in neonates hatching at a time of low food availability.

Introduced Species

Introduced species may affect turtle and crocodilian populations in several ways. Many introduced plant species physically alter habitat important for turtles and crocodilians. The Chinese Tallow Tree is an invasive exotic that is rapidly converting Texas' remaining coastal prairies into brushy woodlands. Invasive range grasses produce dense mats of grass cover that are quite different from the more clumped native grasses to which native turtle species, such as the Texas Tortoise (*Gopherus berlandieri*), are adapted. Introduced aquatic vegetation such as water hyacinth may alter aquatic ecosystems by blocking sunlight available to native aquatic plants upon which turtles feed or that form the basis of natural aquatic food chains.

Introduced predators may present challenges that certain species are ill-adapted to avoid. Perhaps the most insidious ex-

Both feral and pet cats pose threats to hatchling turtles.

otic predator of young turtles is one that many of us overlook but with which we are intimately familiar—our domestic house cats. Both feral cats and their well-fed counterparts that people regard as pets may take a toll on turtle populations, particularly hatchlings, when allowed to roam free.

The invasive and introduced Red Fire Ants (*Solenopsis invicta*) have been implicated in declines of some species; however, comparison baseline data of turtle population densities prior to the introduction of these ants is unavailable. It is thought that adult turtles and crocodilians are largely unaffected by fire ant predation, but that their nests and hatchlings may be particularly susceptible.

Other species may compete with turtles and crocodilians directly for access to food, shelter, and territories. Of particular interest are those cases in which the introduced species is closely related to a similarly adapted native species. Although this phenomenon is not well studied in turtles or crocodilians, it has been studied in great detail in lizards. One well-studied example of such a species pair involves the native Green Anole (*Anolis carolinensis*) and the introduced Brown Anole (*Anolis sagrei*). In the absence of Brown Anoles, Green Anoles utilize parts of their habitat ranging from the ground up into the treetops. However, when faced with competition from Brown

Pseudemys nelsoni is a species that has been introduced from Florida into Texas waters. It remains unclear what impact this introduction has had on native turtle populations in the San Marcos area. Highlands Co., Florida.

Trachemys scripta is a turtle native to Texas that has been widely introduced outside its native range and is considered an invasive species throughout much of the world. Introductions of this species in the upper Rio Grande system threaten its close relative *Trachemys gaigeae* with genetic pollution from hybridization. Chambers Co., Texas.

Anoles, the Green Anole mostly abandons the ground and lower shrubs, retreating (or being forced) into the mid-to-upper branches of trees. This principle is known in ecology as competitive exclusion. Potentially, these sorts of interactions may occur between native Texas River Cooters (*Pseudemys texana*) and the introduced Florida Red-bellied Cooter (*Pseudemys nelsoni*) at Spring Lake in San Marcos. Fortunately, no populations of Spectacled Caiman (*Caiman crocodilus*) have become established in Texas, but were this to occur they could potentially interact with native American Alligators (*Alligator mississippiensis*) in unknown ways.

Effects of Predator Control on Turtles and Turtle Nests

Changes to one level of an ecosystem can have unforeseen cascading effects throughout an ecosystem. Predator control aimed at the removal of large predators, such as mountain lions, coyotes, and bobcats, has resulted in circumstances that have had an indirect negative effect on turtle populations. Large predators can affect populations of small predators in a variety of ways. First, large predators may prey directly on smaller predators. Coyotes are known to prey upon both raccoons and arma-

Raccoons and other medium-sized predators frequently prey on turtles and their nests. Edwards Co., Texas.

In areas of dense raccoon populations, many (most?) turtle nests may be dug up and eaten within a few hours of being laid, such as this nest in Kinney Co., Texas.

dillos, for example. Further, large predators may compete with smaller predators more efficiently for food. Therefore, through both predation and competition, populations of small predators are kept in check by larger ones. These interactions affect turtle populations indirectly because raccoons are well documented as one of the primary predators of turtle nests and nestlings. The removal of large predators from an area has been shown to allow raccoon populations to increase, resulting in an increase in predation on turtle nests. Outside Texas, it will be interesting to see if the introduction of Burmese Pythons (*Python molurus*) into Florida's Everglades will ultimately result in increasing populations of turtles in this region, as these large predators have been documented to be having a serious negative impact on the Everglades' raccoon population.

Effects of the International Trade in Turtle Meat Products

Turtle meat has long been considered a delicacy in many rural parts of the world. For example, the common name "Chicken Turtle" for *Deirochelys reticularia* is in reference to the meat of this turtle supposedly tasting like chicken. As recently as the late 1970s, Florida Gopher Tortoises (*Gopherus polyphemus*) were dug from their burrows and eaten. The first Bolson Tortoise (*Gopherus flavomarginatus*) known to science was in the form of a shell of a turtle that had been killed and eaten by local ranchers in northern Mexico. The killing of turtles for food by rural Americans has been implicated in declines of many US species including but not limited to Diamondback Terrapins (*Malaclemys terrapin*), Alligator Snapping Turtles (*Macrochelys temminckii*), and various species of sea turtles.

However, this problem is much more severe in the countries of Southeast Asia, where wild populations of virtually every native species of turtle have declined to the point that local turtle populations cannot meet the demand for their meat. For example, in 2011, a single market in Bangladesh butchered close to 100,000 turtles for consumption during a single religious festival! Beginning in the late 1990s and early 2000s, Asian turtle markets increasingly have turned to international sources for turtle meat, including the United States. As an example, between 2002 and 2005, 250,000 wild-caught turtles were exported to China from a single airport in Texas. A study by the World Chelonian Trust during that same period estimates that 31.8 MILLION(!) turtles were exported out of the United States. The only positive in this estimate is that approximately 97% were farm-raised individuals of a single species, the Pond Slider (*Trachemys scripta*), and that this number includes both specimens destined for the global pet trade as well as for Asian food markets. Regardless, 3% of 31.8 million is still almost 1 million wild turtles exported from the United States in that time frame. Given the long life span and low reproduction rates of turtles, harvests at these levels have the potential to cause devastating crashes in wild populations.

When these facts caught the attention of turtle enthusiasts as well as wildlife biologists, groups began to push for legislation regulating or prohibiting the commercial harvest of wild turtles in the United States. One unique challenge to complicate this situation was that turtle populations were not well studied prior to commercial harvest, so baseline data were not available to enable biologists to determine the effects of these harvests. The situation was studied by game agencies across the southeastern United States, ultimately resulting in regulations controlling the commercial harvest of most turtle species throughout the region.

Today, Texas allows the commercial harvest of only four turtle species: the Snapping Turtle (*Chelydra serpentina*), the Pond Slider (*Trachemys scripta*), and both species of native softshell turtles (*Apalone mutica* and *A. spinifera*). These animals may only be harvested from private waters with express written permission from landowners, and no turtles may be taken from public waters.

Collection for the Pet Trade as Cause of Decline

Although the collecting of turtles from the wild has been implicated in the declines of some species, the impacts of collecting on most species of turtles are either poorly known or completely unknown. Perhaps the most well-known case of collecting causing a reduction in local populations of turtles in Texas was the historic collection of Texas Tortoises (*Gopherus berlandieri*) for the pet trade in the 1950s and 1960s. However, even with this case, the specific effects of the removal of the estimated thousands of individuals from Texas remain unclear and undocumented. The trade in this species was one of the first closed by the state of Texas, with the placement of it on the state threatened species list in the early 1970s. Declines in box turtle (*Terrapene* spp.) populations have also been attributed to the pet trade, and although it is certain that the removal of adult box turtles from wild populations can have severe consequences, particularly as very few hatchling box turtles ever survive to adulthood, the actual impacts of collection are difficult to tease away from the various other causes of mortality for these species (including road mortality, habitat loss and fragmentation, and nest predation). Today, only a few common native turtles may be collected commercially, and of these typically only Pond Sliders (*Trachemys scripta*) are made available to the pet trade, as Snapping Turtles (*Chelydra serpentina*) and softshells (*Apalone* spp.) rather aggressively defend themselves by biting and do not make good pets. In addition, the relative proportions of these animals entering the pet trade are overshadowed by the numbers entering the meat trade. While there may be impacts to local populations in these species, the impacts or potential impacts of these collections remain largely speculative but should be studied further. Furthermore, these species of turtles reach sexual maturity in a few years and produce multiple clutches of eggs during the year, making their populations more tolerant of collection pressures than are most other species of turtles. Today, through tracking of commercial nongame dealers, we know that thousands of native turtles (this total includes data for several species) enter the commercial trade annually (either as pets or as food items for humans)—numbers that at first glance may seem alarming but which have been rather consistent since permitting has been implemented, suggesting a degree of sustainability for these prolific turtles. However, many researchers have argued that monitoring programs for these species are insufficient as they rely primarily on harvest numbers rather than actual surveys of turtle populations. This problem needs further study, and the Texas Parks and Wildlife Department (TPWD) should be prepared to close the commercial trade in turtles if harvest or future survey data indicate declines in their populations.

Impacts of Fisheries Practices upon Turtle Species

Fisheries practices have been implicated in declines of numerous turtle species, ranging from incidental take from sportfishing with live bait, to death of turtles from unattended trotlines, to reduction in populations of Diamondback Terrapins (*Mala-*

Fishhooks are difficult to remove from the mouths of most turtles, and lines are often simply cut off, leaving the hook in place. The turtles are left to starve, such as this *Sternotherus carinatus*, Pike Co., Arkansas.

Close-up of fishhook embedded in the jaw of a *Sternotherus carinatus*, Pike Co., Arkansas.

clemys terrapin) from crab traps, to impacts on sea turtle populations associated with shrimp trawling nets.

Sport and recreational anglers frequently hook turtles when using live bait such as earthworms and minnows. Many species of turtles include these bait species in their diets, and as hooked bait worms or minnows cannot escape, these baits make a tempting meal for a turtle. Although turtles may frequently only nibble at bait on a hook and escape without being hooked, those that are hooked present a problem for even the most ethical angler, as it is extremely difficult to remove a hook from the mouth of a turtle, especially if the hook was swallowed deeply into the turtle's throat. Extracting a hook from a turtle's throat requires the use of needle-nosed pliers, and turtles often bite and close their hooked beaks, making extraction difficult. In many cases, anglers simply cut the line above the hook, leaving the hook embedded in the turtle's mouth or throat. While the hook may eventually work its way out of the animal's mouth, in most cases it does not, and the turtle dies as a result of starvation or infection. The actual impacts of sportfishing to turtle populations are unknown.

Trotline fishing for catfish presents a similar problem as does sportfishing. The problems associated with this practice are often compounded by unscrupulous individuals leaving trotlines unattended for periods of weeks instead of removing the lines when they are finished with them. One study of Alligator Snapping Turtle (*Macrochelys temminckii*) populations in East Texas rivers found that these turtle populations were strongly and inversely correlated with the number of trotlines present in a particular stretch of river—in short, the more trotlines present, the fewer turtles present.

Crab trapping in coastal estuaries has been implicated in population declines of Diamondback Terrapins (*Malaclemys terrapin*) throughout their range. Crab traps are typically submerged in coastal marshes and estuaries inhabited by both crabs and turtles. As the crabs are a natural prey of the terrapins, terrapins may enter crab traps in search of an easy meal, only to drown in the traps when they cannot escape. This problem can be avoided by placing a 4.5 × 1 cm rectangle in the mouth of the crab trap, which allows crabs but not turtles to enter the trap. This preventative measure should be more widely adopted in order to protect these unique and beautiful turtles.

Shrimping nets have long been implicated in sea turtle declines, as sea turtles are readily scooped into these trawling nets, where they become entangled and drown. There are specially designed Turtle Excluder Devices, or TEDs, that legally must be used with all trawling nets in US waters and help to prevent turtles from being drowned. However, their effectiveness is unclear, and dead sea turtles continue to wash ashore regularly on Texas beaches. Whether this is a case of the TEDs not working as advertised, reluctance of shrimp trawlers to use them or use them properly, or both, remains unclear.

Historic Declines and Recovery of the American Alligator

Beginning with European colonization of the southeastern United States and continuing through the late 1960s, the American Alligator (*Alligator mississippiensis*) was indiscriminately hunted for its hide, meat, and parts. In addition, alligators were hunted out of largely unfounded fears that they would prey upon livestock. By the late 1960s, alligator populations were so decimated that many people believed that they would never recover, and they were listed as an endangered species in 1967 by the US Fish and Wildlife Service (USFWS). In 1969, Texas followed suit and provided complete protection for the American Alligator.

With the complete cessation of legal alligator hunting, these prolific animals rapidly began to repopulate the landscape, re-colonizing virtually all available habitats throughout their former range. As alligator populations increased, states, including Texas, established monitoring programs and funded research to better understand their population dynamics and growth rates and to create management plans. In 1984, Texas began harvesting wild alligators under sustainable yield principles. In 1987, the USFWS removed the species from the endangered species list, pronouncing it fully recovered. Through the cooperation of state and federal agencies, the recovery of the American Alligator is one of the great success stories of the nation's endangered species program.

Although American Alligator populations are demonstrably secure, some related animals such as some caimans and crocodiles remain threatened and endangered. For this reason, the legal trade in alligator skins and products continues to be governed by the USFWS and by the international treaty, the Convention in the Trade of Endangered Species (CITES). These measures have been established to ensure that endangered species with skin similar in appearance to the American Alligator remain protected.

Impacts of Sport Hunting on American Alligator Populations in Texas

As a sustainable resource, alligators are important to local economies, and the revenue provided to landowners through sport hunting and the harvest of alligators serves as incentive to protect and manage alligator habitat. Responsible recreational and commercial harvest is a critical component of effective habitat management, guaranteeing the future of alligators and many other species that share its habitat. The management plan for the American Alligator in Texas involves various harvest and management techniques that have been established for the species based upon extensive research conducted primarily in Louisiana. Wildlife biologists with TPWD monitor the Texas alligator populations in 22 core counties and on certain specific public and private properties by means of aerial nesting surveys and nighttime spotlight counts along specified transects. Three-year average nest counts, the percentage of adult alligators, and research-based estimates of sustainable yield harvest rates are used to generate harvest recommendations, which in turn are used to determine the number of alligator tags issued to landowners. The number of individual alligators harvested on a property is based on acreage and type of habitat owned. Annual harvest records are kept, documenting size, sex, county of take, and harvest date. These records allow TPWD to monitor population trends in the species, and all aspects of the alligator program are carefully monitored. Contact TPWD or search their website for more details.

OBSERVATION AND COLLECTION OF TURTLES AND CROCODILIANS
Observation of Turtles and Crocodilians

The easiest way to observe both aquatic turtles and crocodilians is to search for basking animals perched on rocks, logs, stumps, or snags that are partially submerged. This process is greatly aided by a quality pair of binoculars. Many basking turtles and alligators are exceedingly wary and may dive into the water at first sight of a potential predator—which, from a turtle's perspective, includes humans. To search for turtles and alligators in this manner, approach the banks of a body of water slowly and carefully, scanning all available basking sites through binoculars. Once a basking animal is spotted, closer approach may be attempted. First, take note of the immediate landscape, hillsides, and tree cover bordering the body of water. Next, plan an approach in such a way as to maximize your cover as you stalk into closer range. Move slowly and steadily along your planned approach, avoiding rapid or jerky movements and sudden stops that are likely to cause the animal to flee. In this manner, one can often approach close enough to observe the animal undisturbed, make note of important field marks to aid in identification, and possibly observe the animal interacting with others of its own or a different species.

Although observing aquatic species of turtles is most readily accomplished by looking for basking individuals perched on logs, to really appreciate their daily activity cycle may require an observer to take up snorkeling or scuba diving. This method is particularly useful for observing turtles inhabiting clear-water springs and streams. Unfortunately, most bodies of water in Texas inhabited by turtles are quite murky, and much of the details of their daily lives remain unobserved. Although American Alligators (*Alligator mississippiensis*) have only rarely been implicated in attacks on humans, care should be taken whenever one encounters one of these animals while swimming! Perhaps fortunately, most alligator populations in Texas inhabit murky waters of the coastal plains and lower river floodplains that are largely unsuited for snorkeling.

Terrestrial species, particularly box turtles (*Terrapene* spp.), may frequently be encountered on cool spring days by searching under cover objects such as rocks, logs, boards, corrugated sheet metal, or even trash items. Although these are the turtles most commonly encountered in such situations, other species may be encountered in similar fashion, particularly if near water. As temperatures warm, these turtles will begin to go about their daily foraging activities and may be encountered as they wander about the landscape. By observing from a distance, many details of these turtles' behavior can be observed, including courtship, mating, egg laying, territorial conflict, and feeding.

During hot weather some turtles (particularly mud and musk turtles in the genera *Kinosternon* and *Sternotherus*, respectively) and the American Alligator (*Alligator mississippiensis*) adopt a nocturnal activity pattern. To observe these species in their activity cycles, one must search for them at night with the aid of a bright flashlight. The development of lighting technology in the past 10 years continues to make this easier. Today, one no longer must carry a bulky flashlight running on four D-cell batteries to achieve high-intensity lighting—in fact, a modern high-intensity LED flashlight may fit into the palm of your hand and produce light four to five times as intense as the old D-cell varieties. With the aid of such light, one may search out waterways and ponds for these animals. Alligators may be readily detected by their red eye-shines. Hold the light against the side of your head near your eyes and pan the light back and forth across a body of water in suspected alligator habitat. If the light strikes the eyes of an alligator, the alligator's eyes will reflect back to you as a red eye-shine. While searching ponds and

Field notes should be written with permanent ink on quality paper. The blank journals available from many booksellers serve this purpose very nicely.

streams at night for actively foraging turtles, one may also encounter sleeping specimens of diurnal species, often perched on branches and in brush tangles near or just beneath the water's surface.

To enhance your knowledge of turtles and crocodilians, it is often helpful to maintain a journal in which to record useful information on your observations. Location, date, time, temperature, percent cloud cover, moon phase (for nocturnal observations), species, behavior, and number of individuals observed are all important information. Location data should be as specific as possible—latitude and longitude can be recorded either by means of a handheld GPS unit or from careful examination of mapping programs such as Google Earth. This information can be reviewed to assist future searches for a particular species, allowing the observer to rely not on faulty memory but on documented data. Furthermore, the information contained in such journals can be used to assist researchers to understand and target your local turtle and crocodilian populations.

Turtle and Crocodilian Photography
Most of the photographs in this book were taken with a single lens reflex (SLR) camera with a macro or telephoto lens and

accessory flash or flashes. Those images taken prior to 2006 were shot with film cameras, but all of the recent photos were taken with digital SLRs. Focal length for the macro lenses used ranged from 40 to 105 mm, while telephoto focal lengths typically ranged from 200 to 400 mm. Use of a flash allows images to be taken at a high F-stop, resulting in increased depth of field. Some of the posed photos were taken with two separate off-camera flashes mounted with diffusers, while most of the in situ photographs were taken with ambient light that may or may not have been supplemented with a single flash—either off camera or the "pop-up" flash integral to the camera.

When one photographs a turtle that has been collected, the first consideration for a quality photograph is a suitable background. Moss beds, leaves, and other nonreflective surfaces that are relatively simple allow the animal to stand out. Turtles should be posed in such a way that their faces point slightly toward the camera. For most turtles, the photo session now becomes a waiting game, as a photographer must exhibit extreme patience while waiting for the turtle to extend its head, neck, and limbs. This may be facilitated by placing the camera on a tripod and focusing the lens on the turtle. Use of a remote or cable shutter release may allow you to sit back comfortably in a lawn chair while you wait for the turtle to come out of its shell. For a particularly shy species or individual, you might even want to bring along a book to read while you wait!

Alternatively, some aquatic species can be successfully and easily photographed in a naturalistic aquarium setting. When doing so, care must be taken so that any glare from the glass of the aquarium is minimized. We have found that holding the flash above the aquarium and shooting the light of the flash straight down into the water gives the most natural-appearing results. Mud and musk turtles (*Kinosternon* spp. and *Sternotherus* spp., respectively) are most easily photographed in this manner, as are smaller map turtles (*Graptemys* spp.), juvenile sliders (*Trachemys* spp.), and juvenile cooters (*Pseudemys* spp.).

Perhaps even more rewarding is to photograph turtles and crocodilians in the field with a telephoto lens as they go about their natural activities. When doing so, slowly and carefully approach a turtle or crocodilian that has been spotted. Rapid or jerky movements are far more likely to elicit a flight response in an animal than are slow, gradual movements. Carefully watch the animal during this process, looking for changes in body posture that indicate it is becoming nervous of your approach. Take photos throughout your approach—with digital photography there is no film to waste, and a distant shot may be able to be cropped into a respectable image. These initial distant shots may also be discarded if you are able to get better, closer images. Occasionally and with practice you may find that some species allow you to approach close enough for in situ macro shots.

One final note regarding photographs is that they are becoming increasingly more accepted for use as vouchers to document the occurrence of a particular species in a particular location. Although a photograph contains far less data than does a specimen, and in many ways is a very inadequate substitute for a specimen, photography is far more accessible to the general public than is preparing and preserving scientific specimens. Photography also is the only way that an unpermitted individual can document the occurrence of a threatened or endangered species. Photographs, with accompanying data, can then be submitted to an appropriate research museum database or online database system, such as the Herps of Texas project (part of iNaturalist.org), and may be used to document the occurrence of that species at a particular time and location. Remember, if you encounter a species in an area where it has not been documented previously, then it should be documented! If it's not documented, it's just a story!

Collection of Turtles

Because the capture and harvest of the American Alligator (*Alligator mississippiensis*) is governed under specific TPWD regulations (see below), we do not provide a discussion for the capture of these large animals. Large adult alligators present extreme danger when handled, and untrained individuals should not attempt to capture or handle alligators in excess of about 1.2 m (4 ft.), and then only under regulations described in the section below, "Legal Aspects of Collecting Turtles and Crocodilians."

Although collecting animals from the wild is becoming more controversial, we feel strongly that whether or not to collect should be a personal choice (provided collecting is done in a legal, responsible, and limited manner). Many people find col-

Aquatic turtles can often be captured with the aid of a long-handled, wide-mouthed net, particularly if one is willing to get wet. Photo by Marla P. Hibbitts.

lecting for a personal captive collection to be more rewarding than purchasing a turtle from a store because maintaining an animal that has been caught in its natural environment often brings back the memories of "the chase." With turtles, it is important to be mindful of the potential specimen's complex natural history and dietary needs. Also one should collect only those species that one is prepared to house as an adult. It is important to remember that many turtle species are extremely long-lived and that a turtle keeper may find him or herself responsible for ensuring the well-being of a turtle for several decades or more. Further, it is important to observe the local, state, and federal laws when collecting in the wild. In Texas it is required that a collector has a permit issued by the state or federal government or a Texas hunting license to collect nongame species. Even with these permits it is important to recognize that certain laws are strictly enforced, and select animals cannot be captured without special state and federal permits. The reader should become familiar with requirements by contacting the TPWD (www.tpwd .state.tx.us) for more information.

Turtles moving about on land can be captured quite easily by hand (note, care should be taken when handling turtles, see discussion below), as they are stereotypically slow-moving animals. Capturing aquatic turtles, on the other hand, often presents quite a challenge. Many aquatic species are quite wary and are more capable swimmers than are most herpetologists. The capture of many species is greatly facilitated by the use of nets or various types of turtle traps. Simple wide-mouthed fishing nets with a small mesh bag can be used to scoop turtles from the water when they are observed foraging on the bottom. When one wishes to attempt to net a turtle that is basking, approaching with most of your body and the net underwater is most likely to be successful. Slowly approach with just your eyes and nose above the waterline, net extended toward the basking turtle. If you are lucky, the turtle may not dive off its basking site until you have the net positioned beneath it. We have found that this method is most successful with younger turtles—mature specimens have learned not to trust strange objects moving toward them in the water! Occasionally, a basking turtle may allow a sufficiently close approach in this manner so that it is possible to grab the turtle by hand. Turtles may also occasionally be captured using seine nets, whereby two people pull a long net through the water between them. It is, however, difficult to use this method to capture turtles on purpose. On the other hand, seining is often quite an enjoyable activity for an aquatic biologist, as one never knows what species may turn up in the net.

Diurnal aquatic turtles may also be collected at night by searching for turtles sleeping in snags and on logs near their basking sites. Typically, these turtles will rest just under the water's surface so that they may periodically extend their necks to the surface for air. Searching for turtles in this manner is most easily facilitated by using a boat with an electric motor or paddles. Gently navigate the boat toward a submerged deadfall with one person lying in the bow. Using a light, preferably a headlamp, search to determine if there are any sleeping turtles present and then reach down into the water and grab them.

Softshell turtles (*Apalone* spp.) may frequently be found partially buried in sandbars in rivers. Often, a softshell's tracks remain present under the water's surface, and these can be followed until one spots a depression or divot created by the turtle partially burying itself in the sandy bottom of the stream or river. Due to the slippery nature and difficulty in grasping one of these turtles, a hand net may be used to facilitate capture.

Trapping turtles involves the use of two kinds of traps: basking traps and hoop traps. A basking trap is simply a basket that is placed under a likely turtle basking site. To use a basking trap, one should observe sites that turtles are using for basking. One can then fasten the basking trap beneath the basking site (typically with the aid of a boat). Allow an hour or more to pass, and then return to the basking site. When the turtles dive off the basking site back into the water, some of them may dive into your basket, allowing them to be captured. Hoop traps are much like minnow traps, only much larger. They consist of a cylindrical hoop of net or wire with a large funnel on one or both ends. Typically, the trap is baited with sardines, dog food, or canned mollusks, which attract foraging turtles. Care should be taken to ensure that the top portion of the trap is above the waterline, so that trapped turtles can come up for air, and that the trap is firmly anchored, so that it cannot roll into deeper water. Typically, such a trap is set out overnight or for a period of several days and should be checked regularly. It must be noted that the use of turtle traps is prohibited on public waters in Texas without a permit from the TPWD.

As a final note on collecting, the advantage of collecting turtles is that one group or another can be collected on all except the coldest days of the winter. Unlike snakes, which tend to retreat deep underground in winter, at least some turtles can be found near the surface under cover objects or basking on warm days throughout the year in Texas.

To assist university research we collect voucher specimens for proof of location or season. We make these collections sparingly and with complete scientific information recorded and archived. Usually only one or two voucher specimens per study area per season per objective are required. For many museum collection purposes we generally attempt to find what are referred to as DOR (dead on road) individuals so that we will not have to kill an individual. Although turtle shells are brittle and may be crushed by a car's tires, at least some fresh DOR specimens are often in good enough shape to be prepared for museum storage. Instances may also occur in which animals vouchered are kept alive by the collector or in one of the museum collections, and upon its natural expiration the animal is prepared and stored permanently in one of the museum collections. Although photographs may be vouchered, in most cases a specimen is preferred, as a specimen provides much more inherent data than does a photograph. Today, it is increasingly important to take tissue samples for DNA work—these tissues should be taken prior to fixation in preservation media. In all cases the collector should keep copious field notes and, whenever possible, make them available to local herp groups for publication in newsletters when something new or noteworthy appears.

Legal Aspects of Collecting Turtles and Crocodilians

A variety of recent legislation has been enacted in Texas that now applies to the collecting and trade of native nongame species (including turtles and crocodilians). These laws also apply to the importation of the same species. In addition to state laws, local ordinances also govern the take and maintenance of certain turtle and crocodilian species. These laws vary according to locality and are in a continual state of flux. It is important to know the city, county, state, and federal laws pertaining to the area where an individual is collecting.

The legal aspects of collecting and maintaining animals can be complex. This becomes more complex when importing turtles and crocodilians, purchasing imported animals, moving animals from place to place, or simply maintaining animals in captivity. In our discussion we will not include legal issues for importing foreign and exotic animals since these animals really do not have a place in a field guide for Texas. However, introduced species can displace native species in their natural habitat if released or accidentally escape from a cage into the environment. We do not condone the purposeful introduction of any nonnative species into Texas habitats.

Legislation and regulations have been established to provide protection and guidelines regarding collecting, dealing in, and maintaining reptiles and amphibians. Some of these have been written for the protection of rare and endangered species, some for the protection of habitats, and some for the protection of the keeper and the public. If you are planning to collect turtles or crocodilians it is vital that you set your objectives and know your legal position before you attempt to collect, import, or keep any reptiles or amphibians.

Several levels of legal jurisdiction exist with which one must be familiar. Ignoring these may result in a citation, and should one be found guilty, a fine; in cases involving threatened and endangered species, one may face jail. Discussion of these levels of jurisdiction follows.

LOCAL LAWS These include cities and counties. Most of these governments have various ordinances concerning collecting and (or) keeping turtles and crocodilians. Many jurisdictions ban various types of reptiles in personal homes (in particular, large or venomous snakes, lizards, or crocodilians, as well as invasive exotics). Inquire with the local governments regarding the animals before you collect and (or) keep them. The local humane society may be the logical place to begin. Follow this with a phone call to the local animal control officer.

TEXAS STATE LAWS At present in the state of Texas a hunting license is required to collect most turtles for personal use. Most species may be collected for only noncommercial purposes and in limited numbers (fewer than six). Only four species (the Snapping Turtle [*Chelydra serpentina*], the Pond Slider [*Trachemys scripta*], the Smooth Softshell [*Apalone mutica*], and the Spiny Softshell [*Apalone spinifera*]) may be collected in excess of this figure, and then only with a commercial collecting permit. Contact the TPWD for additional details.

American Alligators (*Alligator mississippiensis*) are regulated under a variety of special permits, including the following.

- Alligator Farmer Permits, which authorize a person to hold live alligators in captivity for commercial purposes, including the selling of alligator eggs, hide, meat, or other parts.
- Alligator Import Permits, which entitle a person to import alligators or alligator parts into Texas.

- Alligator Export Permits, which authorize a farmer to export live alligators.
- Alligator Nuisance Control Permits, which allow permittees to contract with landowners to remove nuisance alligators and process or sell them, including their hides, meat, or other parts.

Again, interested individuals should contact the TPWD directly for additional details.

In addition, alligators may be hunted under the authority of a resident or nonresident hunting license. In select "core counties" and on certain properties in other counties a person must possess a valid CITES tag in order to hunt alligators legally. In these core counties, CITES tags are issued by the TPWD to landowners following a site inspection and evaluation of the property and its alligator population. Alligator season in these counties and properties runs from September 10 to 30. For information about tag issuance and requirements, contact the J. D. Murphree Wildlife Management office.

In all other Texas counties (noncore counties), open season on alligators runs from April 1 to June 30. Alligators may not be taken on any property where alligators were taken during the September season. In these counties, the bag limit on alligators is one alligator per person per year, and alligators may be taken on private properties only. Alligators in public waters may be taken by any lawful means except the use of firearms, provided the person taking the alligator and the device used to take the alligator are on private property adjoining the public waters. Upon harvesting an alligator, a person must immediately complete a wildlife resource document (WRD), available online from the TPWD; the WRD shall accompany the alligator until it is permanently tagged with a CITES tag. Within 72 hours of harvest, a completed alligator hide tag report (also available online from the TPWD) must be mailed to the TPWD along with a check or money order for the CITES hide tag fee (currently, US$21). Once the tag arrives in the mail, the alligator must be permanently tagged with the CITES tag. Alligators may be taken only between one-half hour before sunrise until sunset. In addition, the TPWD describes detailed acceptable means and methods of take. See the TPWD for more details.

FEDERAL LAWS Aside from regulating the collection of federally threatened and endangered turtle and crocodilian species, the US government allows the individual states to regulate their own native species. However, in cases where violation of state laws involves the transport of animals across state lines, federal law is violated (the Lacey Act), and federal law enforcement may take jurisdiction.

The Lacey Act basically states that acquisition of any plant or animal in violation of any sovereign state's law is a violation of federal law. The Endangered Species Act is designed to protect rare and endangered animals. The US Fish and Wildlife Service (Department of the Interior) can provide a listing of currently recognized endangered amphibians and reptiles.

The Injurious Wildlife Act concerns animals such as mongooses, walking catfish, venomous snakes and lizards, and certain toxic amphibians. This act is administered by the Department of Agriculture.

Finally, the US Food and Drug Administration (USFDA) prohibits the sale of turtle eggs or live turtles with a carapace length less than 10.2 cm (4 in.). Exceptions allow for the sale of live turtles for "scientific, educational, or exhibitional purposes, other than use as pets," as well as for the sale of live turtles and eggs "intended for export only." These measures were enacted as a measure aimed at preventing food poisoning by *Salmonella* bacteria, which may occur on the skin of turtles, lizards, snakes, crocodilians, and birds.

Permits and Collecting Turtles and Crocodilians in Texas

The permit and legal issues of hunting and collecting turtles, like with other game and nongame animals, is always in a state of evolution, so we recommend that the reader contact the TPWD for current information. The following gives some points taken from the guidelines of a recent set of Texas Parks and Wildlife Outdoor Annual Hunting and Fishing Regulations (2013–2014).

- Turtles are considered to be nongame animals.
- A hunting license is required of any person, regardless of age, who hunts any animal or bird in this state (Texas).
- A hunting license is required to take nonprotected turtles.

Nongame species in Texas have been further categorized as to the number that can be kept in captivity. The species that are not listed as threatened or endangered have now been put on either the "White List" or the "Black List." Species on the Black List may not be sold and can only be kept in quantities of six or fewer. Species on the White List may be sold, and 25 or fewer may be kept without a nongame dealer permit. The permit is needed when maintaining more than 25 White List animals or when selling these animals. The only species of turtle in Texas that are on the White List and that may be utilized commercially are the Snapping Turtle (*Chelydra serpentina*), the Pond Slider (*Trachemys scripta*), the Smooth Softshell (*Apalone mutica*), and the Spiny Softshell (*Apalone spinifera*).

Legislation passed in 2011 allows collection of turtles from public right-of-ways and waters for noncommercial use only. This partially reversed legislation that had been passed in 2007, which prohibited all take of nongame species from public right-of-ways and waters. Current regulations require a person to park his or her vehicle completely off the pavement and wear a reflective vest with 930 cm^2 (144 in.^{2}) of reflective material on both front and back; regulations also prohibit the shining of lights from the vehicle to assist the search. Note, none of this legislation makes it illegal to search for these species for legitimate photographic purposes; however, be advised that it is likely that a turtle photographer may be suspected of collecting. When searching for turtles to photograph along right-of-ways or on public waters, consider making a courtesy telephone call to your local game warden.

In addition, we recommend that the reader refer to the current regulations for status of resident and nonresident collectors and general hunting and fishing regulations. For further questions or more information contact the TPWD Law Enforcement Office at 1-800-792-1112 (toll free) or 512-389-4800, Monday through Friday, 8:00 a.m. to 5:00 p.m. (except on holidays).

Threatened, Endangered, and Protected Nongame Species

It is unlawful for any person to hunt and (or) collect threatened, endangered, or protected nongame species. To sell or purchase goods made from threatened or endangered species, proper documentation must accompany the goods. For a complete current list of threatened and endangered species, and regulations relating to breeding threatened and endangered species, contact the TPWD. There may be other more encompassing special federal or CITES regulations, and any turtle hunter or collector should be aware of these.

MAINTENANCE OF TURTLES AND CROCODILIANS
Maintenance of Turtles and Crocodilians in Captivity

Maintaining turtles in captivity can be rewarding, and some species can be kept relatively easily. On the other hand, most crocodilians reach sufficiently large sizes that maintaining them in captivity should be left to experienced professionals in zoological parks and specialized crocodilian farms. Only the smallest species of crocodilian, such as the dwarf caimans (*Paleosuchus* spp.) of South America, are small enough as adults to make suitable captives in vivarium culture. Furthermore, the keeping of American Alligators (*Alligator mississippiensis*) is prohibited by law in Texas. Therefore, the remainder of this discussion will focus on maintaining turtles in captivity. Remember to follow all laws governing the keeping of Texas native species when acquiring turtles for captive husbandry.

Turtles can make fascinating pets. Some species require relatively small space, and their maintenance requirements can be easily met in homes, apartments, or offices. Other species can be allowed to roam freely in backyard enclosures, provided measures are taken to prevent their escape. Smaller aquatic species, such as mud and musk turtles (*Kinosternon* and *Sternotherus* spp., respectively) can be housed in medium to large (76–208 L; 20–55 gal.) aquaria with a branch or float provided for basking. Larger species may require larger aquaria or enclosures, with many species attaining sufficiently large sizes as adults (such as the cooters, *Pseudemys* spp.) that they are best maintained in outdoor pools or tanks.

Another consideration in maintaining most turtles in captivity is that most species require daily exposure to full-spectrum lights containing ultraviolet light. Ultraviolet light is necessary for the turtle's skin cells to synthesize vitamin D, and vitamin D is necessary for the metabolism of calcium and the production of strong bones (humans produce vitamin D in a similar manner). Vitamin D may also be provided with the turtle's food as a supplement and should be for most captives—however, supplementation will likely provide adequate levels of vitamin D for only nonbasking species, whereas species that are active baskers will still require full-spectrum lighting in order to meet their needs completely. Turtles maintained outside in enclosures or ponds may meet their needs for vitamin D production naturally from sunlight.

Requirements for keeping turtles in captivity vary with their life histories, which are different for each species. Terrestrial species such as box turtles (*Terrapene* spp.) are kept most simply in outdoor enclosures. Care must be taken to make the enclosure escape proof—typically by burying fine-mesh wire or aluminum flashing at least 20 cm (8 in.) underground along the edges of their enclosure to prevent digging. Furthermore, turtles are surprisingly capable climbers, and most species are readily capable of climbing a knee-high fence. To prevent escape by climbing, the top of the fence should be bent inward at a 90-degree angle for approximately 20 cm (8 in.). Covered shelters and watering depressions should be provided. Enclosures should be large enough to allow the turtles to choose sunny versus shaded areas, which will allow basking and thermoregulation. The enclosure can be landscaped with rocks, logs, and native vegetation. Leaf litter can be composted in a turtle enclosure, providing them with cover into which they can readily bury themselves. Some turtle keepers may choose to modify their entire backyards as turtle enclosures for terrestrial species. In winter, temperate species of turtles may be allowed to hibernate in composting piles of leaves or they may be brought indoors and maintained in a vivarium setting. One final challenge of maintaining turtles outdoors is predator control. In most urban environments, this may not present a problem, but in suburban and rural settings, a turtle keeper must always be aware of the danger presented by wild predators, particularly raccoons. To avoid the possibility of such predation, fencing or netting can be erected over the enclosure. Design plans for turtle enclosures can be found online or in various resources pertaining to the keeping of box turtles or the various species of tortoise available in the pet trade.

Keeping terrestrial species indoors presents greater chal-

lenges than does keeping them outdoors. Terrestrial turtles require large enclosures with ample air flow, a temperature gradi-
ent ranging from the lower 20s Celsius (upper 70s Fahrenheit)
on one end of the enclosure to a warm (up to 40 degrees Celsius,
or 90+ degrees Fahrenheit), illuminated basking spot (provided
by an incandescent light bulb) on the other end. While incandescent bulbs provide warmth and will attract a turtle to bask,
they do not produce ultraviolet light—this must be provided
by a fluorescent bulb. Fluorescent bulbs, however, do not provide sufficient heat to encourage the turtle to bask—so neither
light alone is sufficient. A turtle produces a surprising amount
of waste, and their enclosures should be cleaned frequently.

Small aquatic and semiaquatic turtles, as well as young turtles of larger species, may be kept in home aquaria. Perhaps the
first consideration when keeping turtles in an aquarium setting
is filtration. Turtles produce more waste than do fish, so to ensure proper water quality use a filter larger than would be necessary for an aquarium of the same size containing fish. Most
species of turtles will benefit from, and many species require, a
place to climb out of the water and bask. Typically, the aquarium should be maintained with a water level lower than completely full, and rocks, bricks, or branches may be arranged in
such a way as to provide the turtles with the ability to climb
onto them and out of the water. Alternatively, a basking plat-
form can be constructed out of wood or acrylic. Designs for
these can be found in online or print resources pertaining to the
keeping of aquatic turtles. Furthermore, the basking site should
be illuminated with both incandescent and fluorescent lighting,
as described above for keeping terrestrial turtles in a vivarium
setting.

Many species of aquatic turtles will attain sizes too large for
the average home aquarium. These species should be transferred
to outdoor enclosures as they mature. Ponds designed for keeping large ornamental goldfish and koi make excellent structures
for the outdoor maintenance of larger aquatic turtles. As with
an aquarium setting, remember that turtles produce more waste
than do fish and that a correspondingly larger filter will be necessary to keep the water of a turtle pond clean. A backyard turtle pond should also be enclosed by an escape-proof fence, and

efforts should be taken to discourage predation, particularly in suburban and rural settings (as described above for the keeping of terrestrial turtles).

Anyone considering keeping turtles should familiarize themselves with the particulars of that species' diet. Some species may be kept indefinitely on commercially available turtle pellets, while others may ignore these food offerings (particularly predaceous species). The dietary needs of closely related species may differ significantly. For example, the Eastern Box Turtle (*Terrapene carolina*) feeds much more readily on fruits and vegetables than does its western counterpart, the Ornate Box Turtle (*Terrapene ornata*), which is much more predaceous. We recommend that an aspiring turtle keeper search for specialized publications for maintaining a specific species prior to acquiring a turtle for captive husbandry.

Creation of Turtle and Crocodilian Habitat

Those living in rural settings wishing to encourage box turtles or tortoises to visit their yards must first consider removing barriers between their yards and the surrounding habitat. A yard can be landscaped naturally, with cover objects and bathing pools provided aimed at meeting a turtle's needs. However, the home ranges of most terrestrial turtles are sufficiently large that most turtles will, at best, be infrequent visitors to a person's yard.

Those with sufficient land allowing them to construct ponds may attract aquatic turtle species, in particular pond-adapted species like Snapping Turtles (*Chelydra serpentina*) or Pond Sliders (*Trachemys scripta*), simply by constructing a pond and waiting for turtles to find it. Provide ample basking sites in your pond (such as logs or stumps protruding above the water) to encourage turtles to bask and to make them more viewable.

American Alligators (*Alligator mississippiensis*) are sufficiently large and potentially dangerous to human life that efforts should not be taken to attract them close to homes. Landowners with ample acreage who wish to create habitat to attract alligators can also construct ponds on their properties but should do so at a distance from houses and areas frequented by pets. A standard stock tank with a depth of 2 m (6.5 ft.) is sufficient to provide habitat for an alligator. In areas where alligators are common, such as Texas' coastal prairies and marshes, alligators will colonize any suitable body of water in short order.

Handling of Turtles and Crocodilians

Many turtle species can easily be handled simply by picking them up by their shells. In a presumably defensive display, many turtles urinate when picked up, so caution should be taken to ensure that the "business end" of the turtle is pointed away from your body. Many species of turtles will attempt to bite fingers placed near their heads, so care should be taken to grasp their shells from the sides in most cases. A bite from the beak of even a small box turtle (*Terrapene* spp.) can be quite painful!

Softshell (*Apalone* spp.) and snapping turtles (*Chelydra serpentina* and *Macrochelys temminckii*) present special challenges, as both have long necks and are quick to defend themselves by biting. Many older publications suggest that Snapping

Many turtle species can be safely handled by their shells, as shown with this large adult *Pseudemys floridana*. Okeechobee Co., Florida.

Snapping and softshell turtles may be safely handled by grasping the front and rear margins of the carapace as shown with this young adult Apalachicola Alligator Snapping Turtle (*Macrochelys apalachicolae*). Liberty Co., Florida.

Turtles (*Chelydra serpentina*) have long tails that "make good handles"—however, it has been shown that handling a heavy turtle by the tail puts undue strain on its spinal column, and this handling method is now discouraged. Both snapping turtles and softshell turtles (*Apalone* spp.) should be grasped with one hand on the rear margin of the carapace and the other on the front margin of the carapace just behind the head with the fingers pressing on the base of the neck. This will prevent the head from turning far enough back to bite you. Alligator Snapping Turtles (*Macrochelys temminckii*) are a protected species in Texas and should not be handled except under permits issued by the TPWD to individuals such as animal control workers, game wardens, and research biologists. Lifting truly large specimens (in excess of 35 kg, or 75 lb.) of this species should only be done when absolutely necessary, as lifting them by their shells has been known to cause injury. Furthermore, extreme care should be taken in handling this species, as the beak of a large adult is quite capable of removing a person's fingers!

American Alligators (*Alligator mississippiensis*) should not be handled casually and without specific need (such as moving a specimen away from human habitation). Small specimens (un-

Although large adult *Alligator mississippiensis* should not be handled by untrained and unlicensed individuals, small specimens may be safely handled by grasping them firmly at the back of the head and base of the tail. Liberty Co., Florida.

der 1.2 m [4 ft.]) can be picked up with two hands. Grasp the animal firmly from above with one hand at the base of the tail and another on the back of the neck. The handling of larger specimens should be left to animal control specialists or trained biologists.

Much has been made over the years of the dangers of acquiring *Salmonella* infections from handling turtles. *Salmonella* is a bacterium that may cause food poisoning when ingested and is a natural component of the microbial fauna on the skins of many animals, including turtles. In years past, when hatchling turtles were widely available in the pet trade, these turtles were implicated in numerous cases of food poisoning, particularly in young children. Presumably, young children would place the hatchling turtles in their mouths, resulting in poisoning from *Salmonella* bacteria. This has resulted in USFDA regulations banning the sale of turtles under 10 cm (4 in.). To a large degree, these concerns are overblown. Although it is true that turtles (as well as lizards, snakes, crocodilians, and birds) can carry *Salmonella* bacteria on their skins, simply washing your hands (and not putting a turtle in your mouth!) after handling a turtle will prevent the remote possibility of a *Salmonella* infection.

It is also worth noting that the vast majority of annual *Salmonella* infections in the United States result from handling poultry products, including meat and eggs, and the USFDA has not implemented bans on the sale of eggs smaller than 4 inches!

MUSEUM AND PRESERVED SPECIMENS

We do not encourage private individuals to build a collection of preserved turtle or crocodilian specimens. Such specimens are of much greater value when housed in an active research museum and should be deposited in one. However, individuals such as public school teachers or nature center directors may find that keeping preserved examples of local species may be useful for educational purposes. While an individual keeper or collector may on occasion preserve deceased, captive specimens or those specimens found dead on road (DOR), we do not have a section devoted to such preservation techniques. Many references exist that cover these techniques in detail, but we recommend any reader who is interested in contributing preserved specimens to a museum or a teaching collection to visit their local university for advice from a professional museum curator.

It is important to point out that scientific institutions are not necessarily interested in taking specimens from unknown sources. Generally a relationship must be developed with that institution to establish that the information being supplied is accurate and the specimen legally collected. In all cases, complete data on where and when the animals were collected is of paramount importance to the value of the specimen.

SCIENTIFIC AND COMMON NAMES

Taxonomy is the field of biology that categorizes all living things into groups and assigns names to those groups. Originally, this field was primarily involved with simply naming organisms to facilitate communication among biologists speaking different languages. Organisms and groups of organisms were assigned distinct names at different taxonomic levels, with the taxonomic levels ranging from the all-encompassing kingdom level down through increasingly more specific levels of classification until the most specific level, or species, was reached. Biology students may remember learning the mnemonic "King Phillip Came Over For Great Spaghetti," which stands as a device for remembering the ordered taxonomic classification rankings of kingdom, phylum, class, order, family, genus, and species. In recent years, as DNA and biochemical evidence has allowed a deeper understanding of the relationships between various bacteria and eukaryotic organisms (those whose cells possess a nucleus), the rank of domain has superseded kingdom at the top of the classification hierarchy. Perhaps most importantly, within the taxonomic system every species of living thing is assigned a scientific name consisting of the genus name and the specific epithet. This two-part scientific name is the name for a particular species and is a unique combination of names that identifies only that particular species.

An example best illustrates how this naming system works. The Ornate Box Turtle is a readily identifiable species found throughout Texas and is classified as follows.

Domain: Eukarya (name for the group that includes organisms whose cells contain a nucleus)

Kingdom: Animalia (name for the group that includes all animals)

Phylum: Chordata (name for the group that includes vertebrates and their immediate invertebrate relatives)

Class: Chelonia (name for the group of vertebrates possessing a bony shell enclosing the pectoral and pelvic girdles)

Order: Cryptodira (name for the group of turtles that withdraw their heads and necks straight back into their shells)

Family: Emydidae (name for the group that includes the New World pond turtles and relatives)

Genus: *Terrapene* (name for all of the American box turtles)

Species: *Terrapene ornata* (specific name for the Ornate Box Turtle)

Notice that the species name includes the genus name. The specific epithet "*ornata*" is insufficient to completely and specifically identify the Ornate Box Turtle scientifically in much the same way that the name "Robert" is insufficient to specifically identify an individual person; to do so, the last name "Smith" must be added. While with human names there may be multiple Robert Smiths, with scientific names there is only one *Terrapene ornata*, and that name can be applied to only a single species.

Also notice that the genus and species names are italicized. This reflects that these words have been Latinized. Latin was the language of scholars and scientists when the scientific classification system was first created, so it was natural for these scientists to incorporate Latin in their naming, especially because their goal was to create names for organisms that all scientists could understand, regardless of their native tongue. Today, the system of biological nomenclature continues to use Latin or Latinized versions of words from other languages, such as Greek, English, or Spanish, to name organisms. These names are assigned to species using rules outlined in the International Commission on Zoological Nomenclature (ICZN).

Scientific names are often presented followed by the names of their describer and the year in which the species description was published; for example, *Pseudemys gorzugi* Ward, 1984, indicates that the species was described by J. P. Ward in 1984. If the name of the author appears in parentheses, for example, *Chelydra serpentina* (Linnaeus 1758), this indicates that the species as originally described was recognized as belonging to a different genus (in this case, the genus *Testudo*) when it was described.

Some species may be further subdivided into subspecies, sometimes referred to as "pattern classes" or "geographical variants." A subspecies is a geographically identifiable subset of a species that can be identified through examination of the animal's pattern or morphology. Formerly, subspecies were thought to be incipient species, or populations "on their way" to becoming separate species. However, with examination of genetic data it has become clear in recent decades that most named subspecies do not correspond closely with any sort of restrictions in gene flow between populations and typically intergrade broadly with neighboring geographic races. These geographic races may reflect localized adaptations to environmental conditions, but this is not well understood. For Texas' turtles, most described subspecies that occur in the state either represent poorly defined slices of clinal variation within the species (e.g., subspecies in the Ornate Box Turtle, *Terrapene ornata*) or are represented by only a single subspecies in Texas (e.g., only one subspecies of Pond Slider, *Trachemys scripta*, occurs in Texas). No subspecies has been described in the American Alligator (*Alligator mis-*

sissippiensis). For these reasons, we have chosen not to include subspecies descriptions in our species accounts.

While taxonomy may seem fairly straightforward, it is generally deemed desirable for classification and naming of organisms to reflect our basic understanding of how those organisms are related to one another. The study of how organisms are related to one another is termed phylogenetic systematics. The goal of phylogenetic systematics is to use the characteristics of organisms—including morphological, behavioral, and genetic features—to infer the relationships among populations within species, among species, and among groups of the higher taxonomic categories, such as genera, families, and orders. While the field of taxonomy is governed by a system of naming rules, phylogenetic systematics often seems quite chaotic to lay persons, as different scientists may propose conflicting hypotheses of relationships for the groups that they study. These differences are, in fact, quite representative of the scientific process, as over time evidence will mount in favor of one hypothesis of relationships over another, and ultimately a better understanding of the relationships among organisms will result.

Unfortunately, the process of phylogenetic systematics does not always lead to stability in taxonomy, and name changes may occur with some frequency. This process is often trivialized by categorizing phylogenetic systematists as being in one of two camps: "lumpers" or "splitters." Lumpers are those biologists who combine taxonomic groups under a single name, while splitters would be those scientists who split members of a single taxonomic group into two new categories. Perhaps a third group could also be recognized—the "reshufflers"—which would be those researchers who move named groups from one group to another.

This is currently an exciting time to be a phylogenetic systematist, as technological advances allow researchers access to larger and larger fractions of the DNA present in organisms, which in turn allows ever-increasing amounts of data that can be used to infer relationships among groups of organisms. Consequently, the names of species today are in a state of flux, with new taxonomic arrangements being proposed on a regular basis. Compared with other groups, turtle and crocodilian taxonomy has been relatively stable, but as more information becomes available names are likely to change in order to reflect our understanding of their relationships.

Changing taxonomic arrangements presents as much of a challenge for a field guide author as it does for an amateur naturalist interested in keeping track of these names! As an aid to keeping track of these changes, the Society for the Study of Amphibians and Reptiles (SSAR) publishes a standardized names list: *Scientific and Standard English Names of Amphibians and Reptiles of North America North of Mexico, With Comments Regarding Confidence In Our Understanding* (Crother, 2012). Due to the near constant changes in taxonomy, this list is updated periodically online at www.cnah.org. Note that this is only a list of standardized English names and that the scientific names outlined within it are a reflection of the authors' "confidence in understanding" of the relationships.

For this field guide, the most current online version of the SSAR list was used as a primary reference. We deviate from this list primarily in two regards. First, where we feel that insufficient evidence has been presented to split one species into two, we take a conservative approach and recognize the older arrangement. Second, in regards to "standardized" English names, we deviate from the list in cases where an older name is more widely in use and where said standardized name creates confusion. In particular, we differ from the SSAR list as follows.

1. Eastern Box Turtle (*Terrapene carolina*)—recent genetic evidence has been presented that the western populations of Eastern Box Turtles that occur in Texas may be genetically distinct from populations in eastern and southeastern North America. In this case, the western populations would be recognized as the Three-toed Box Turtle (*Terrapene triunguis*). However, turtles from Mississippi and southeastern Louisiana appear phenotypically intermediate between the two populations, suggesting gene flow between them. Furthermore, the genetic analysis suggesting that the two populations are distinct utilized mitochondrial DNA, which is inherited in a maternal fashion and which cannot be used to assess gene flow between populations. Until further evidence becomes available,

we chose to retain Texas populations of Three-toed Box Turtles within the species known as the Eastern Box Turtle, *Terrapene carolina*.

2. Painted Turtle (*Chrysemys picta*)—recent publications have elevated populations of Painted Turtles occurring in northeast Texas, Louisiana, Mississippi, southeast Oklahoma, and Arkansas to full species status, the Southern Painted Turtle (*Chrysemys dorsalis*). However, turtles from southern Illinois, western Kentucky, eastern Tennessee, southern Missouri, and northeast Arkansas are phenotypically intermediate between southern populations regarded as full species and northern and western populations regarded as the more widespread species *Chrysemys picta*. We feel that this phenotypic intergradation likely represents gene flow between these populations, making the recognition of the Southern Painted Turtle as a full species unwarranted.

3. Stinkpot (*Sternotherus odoratus*)—the common name for *Sternotherus odoratus* has long been presented as the "Stinkpot." Because all members of the family Kinosternidae are capable of emitting a foul-smelling musk, this name was changed first to "Common Musk Turtle" to reflect its widespread distribution. However, the SSAR later decided to adopt the name "Eastern Musk Turtle," arguing that the name "Common Musk Turtle" could be interpreted as meaning that it is the most abundant species of musk turtle in any particular area (which it frequently is not). However, this change invites confusion with the similar and related Eastern Mud Turtle (*Kinosternon subrubrum*). Although it is true that all species of kinosternid turtles can emit musk, none do so as readily as *Sternotherus odoratus*, therefore we chose to retain the common name Stinkpot and consider the other two proposed names to be uninformative and confusing.

4. The Ouachita Map Turtle (*Graptemys ouachitensis*)—the common name for *Graptemys ouachitensis* has historically been designated as the "Ouachita Map Turtle," although this species is by no means restricted to the Ouachita River system and is in fact endemic to much of the Mississippi River and its tributaries. However,

the name "Mississippi Map Turtle" has long been used to describe southern populations of the False Map Turtle (*Graptemys pseudogeographica*), making the adoption of this more descriptive name problematic. However, the adoption of the name "Southern Map Turtle" for *Graptemys ouachitensis* is equally problematic, as there are eleven species of map turtles with more southerly distributions than *Graptemys ouachitensis*. Rather than using a name that implies that this species has a more southerly distribution compared with other map turtle species, we chose to use the common name that has been historically associated with the species for the longest period of time, the Ouachita Map Turtle.

The taxonomic status of the various species of cooters (genus *Pseudemys*) remains confused and in need of further research. Some recent research has suggested that species within the River Cooter (*Pseudemys concinna*) complex (including the Texas River Cooter, *Pseudemys texana*, and the Rio Grande Cooter, *Pseudemys gorzugi*) have been oversplit. However, others have noted substantial variation among populations in different river systems in Texas, as well as phenotypic differences between turtles living above and below the Balcones Escarpment in the same river system. Future research may result in the lumping of one or more of these species together or may result in splitting populations and the identification of new species within the complex.

In addition to the problems presented by variation in Texas' cooters, populations of cooters inhabiting streams and rivers of the southeastern coastal plain have been variously assigned to the river cooter complex, the Florida Cooter (*Pseudemys floridana*), the Suwannee Cooter (*Pseudemys suwanniensis*), and the Peninsula Cooter (*Pseudemys peninsularis*). Species boundaries of the various populations of cooters in this region remain poorly resolved, with turtles showing both geographic differences as well as phenotypic differences between those inhabiting rivers versus ponds. Much research is needed to resolve the identities of the various populations of these turtles (some of which may occur in East Texas), and taxonomic changes within these groups are likely to occur in the near future.

One final note worthy of mention regarding taxonomy is a recent trend by some phylogenetic systematists to abandon using the Linnaean ranked names above genus in favor of simply naming clades containing monophyletic groups (groups containing all the descendants of a single common ancestor) of taxa. These scientists argue that categories such as family and order have little value, largely because a family of animals such as turtles is not equivalent to a family of birds or a family of insects. Furthermore, the Linnaean rank system becomes increasingly complicated when one wants to name groups between, for example, families and orders, resulting in categories such as suborders and superfamilies. Rather than concern themselves with deciding whether or not a named taxonomic group represents an order, suborder, superfamily, family, or subfamily, these scientists argue that clades containing monophyletic lineages of groups should simply be given names that stand by themselves. While this trend is gaining popularity among specialists, it has not been widely adopted outside systematics and is not particularly useful for lay persons wishing to understand the general patterns of relationships between groups of organisms.

DICHOTOMOUS KEY
TO TEXAS TURTLES

DICHOTOMOUS KEYS

A dichotomous key is an identification tool used in science. Each step in the key has two possible results (dichotomous means "divided into two parts") and is usually based on morphological characteristics, including shape, scalation, color, and pattern. Keys are most often made to help identify organisms at the species level, but they can be designed to identify them at higher taxonomic levels. Constructing a useable key can be a daunting task. The goal is to produce a user-friendly key applicable in the laboratory and the field. The terminology used in keys can be very specific, and in many cases diagrams and glossaries are necessary to maneuver through a key easily.

Our key is designed to identify examples of living or freshly killed specimens to the species level. Problems may arise when using the key to identify preserved animals, since preservatives affect the size of the animal, change patterns and colors, distort an animal's natural stature, and make it difficult to move limbs. This key addresses only native Texas turtle species and well-documented established exotic species. Because only a single

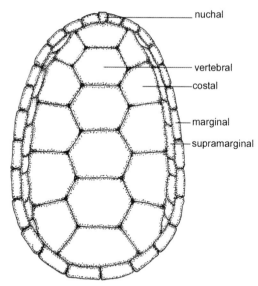

Carapace scutes of a turtle include the nuchal, vertebrals, costals, marginals, and, in some cases, supramarginals.

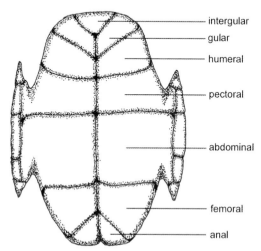

Plastron scutes of a turtle include the gular, humeral, pectoral, abdominal, femoral, anal, and, in some cases, an intergular.

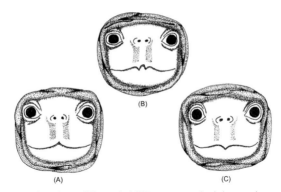

The mouth of a turtle may (A) be notched, (B) have two cusps bordering a notch, or (C) have a single cusp.

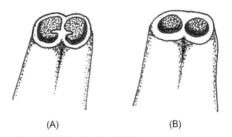

Softshell nostrils may be (A) ridged or (B) unridged.

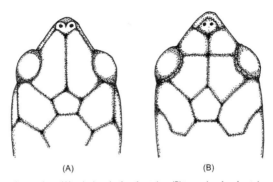

Sea turtles may have (A) a single pair of prefrontals or (B) two pairs of prefrontals.

species of crocodilian occurs naturally in Texas, the American Alligator (*Alligator mississippiensis*) has not been included in this key.

KEY TO TEXAS TURTLES

1. a. Limbs are flippers, only claws present 2
   b. Limbs are normal with digits and claws. 6
2. a. Carapace is covered with leathery skin . . . .
      . . . . .Leatherback Sea Turtle
      Dermochelys coriacea
   b. Carapace is covered with horny plates (scutes) 3
3. a. There are 4 costal scutes on carapace 4
   b. There are 5 costal scutes on carapace 5
4. a. A single pair of prefrontal scales . . . . . . Green Sea Turtle
      Chelonia mydas
   b. Two pairs of prefrontal scales. . . . . .Hawksbill Sea Turtle
      Eretmochelys imbricata
5. a. Each front flipper has one claw . . . .
      . . . . .Kemp's Ridley Sea Turtle
      Lepidochelys kempii
   b. Each front flipper has two claws . . . .
      . . . . Loggerhead Sea Turtle
      Caretta caretta
6. a. Carapace is covered with leathery skin 7
   b. Carapace is covered with horny plates (scutes) 8
7. a. Anterior rim of carapace has tubercles and spines, septum has inward projecting ridge . . . . Spiny Softshell
      Apalone spinifera
   b. Anterior rim of carapace smooth with no tubercles or spines, septum has no projecting ridge . . . .
      . . . . Smooth Softshell
      Apalone mutica
8. a. Plastron hinged (indistinct or distinct) 9
   b. Plastron not hinged 15
9. a. Plastron double hinged 10
   b. Plastron single hinged between pectoral and abdominal scutes. 12
10. a. Triangular-shaped ninth marginal scute with apex extending well above eighth marginal . . . .
       . . . . Yellow Mud Turtle
       Kinosternon flavescens

b. Ninth marginal not extending above eighth marginal . .
. 11

11. a. The first vertebral scute is widely separated from the second marginal. .Eastern Mud Turtle
Kinosternon subrubrum

b. The first vertebral scute touches the second marginal. . .
. . . . Rough-footed Mud Turtle
Kinosternon hirtipes

12. a. Plastron with 10 scutes and an indistinct hinge 13

b. Plastron with 12 scutes and a distinct hinge 14

13. a. Two light stripes on side of head, barbels on chin and
throat . . . . Stinkpot
Sternotherus odoratus

b. Light stripes on side of head absent, barbels on chin
only . . . . Razor-backed Musk Turtle
Sternotherus carinatus

14. a. Carapace flattened, pattern of radiating lines on scutes
constant . . . . .Ornate Box Turtle
Terrapene ornata

b. Carapace domed, pattern not distinct . . . .
. . . . Eastern Box Turtle
Terrapene carolina

15. a. Elephantine rear feet, shovel-like front feet, gular projection. . . . . Texas Tortoise
Gopherus berlandieri

b. Webbed rear feet, webbed or partially webbed front feet,
gular scutes do not project forward. 16

16. a. Tail more than half the carapace length, plastron is small
and cross-shaped 17

b. Tail less than half the carapace length, plastron is large
and not cross-shaped. 18

17. a. Three prominent knobby keels on carapace, row of supramarginals between the marginal scutes and the costal scutes. . . . . Alligator Snapping Turtle
Macrochelys temminckii

b. Three low keels on carapace, no supramarginals present
between the marginal scutes and the costal scutes. . . . . .
. . . . .Snapping Turtle
Chelydra serpentina

18. a. The neck is approximately equal to plastron length, broad forelimb stripe.................Chicken Turtle
    Deirochelys reticularia

    b. The neck is approximately equal to half of plastron length, narrow forelimb stripes.................... 19

19. a. The posterior carapace rim is not serrated............. .... Painted Turtle
    Chrysemys picta

    b. The posterior carapace rim is serrated 20

20. a. The side of head has a wide and prominent orange or red postocular stripe or blotch 21

    b. The side of head has narrow yellow or orange postocular stripes present................................. 22

21. a. A large postocular spot or blotch, circular or oval in shape, the plastron has an intricate central pattern ....Mexican Plateau Slider
    Trachemys gaigeae

    b. A broad elongate postocular bar (sometimes broken into two parts), plastron with paired side blotches.......... ....Pond Slider
    Trachemys scripta

22. a. Carapace with prominent vertebral keel, with low to moderate spine-like projections.................... 23

    b. Carapace with no or slight vertebral keel or with no spine-like projections............................. 28

23. a. Carapace scutes are rough, with concentric ridges; head lacks any stripes .... Diamond-backed Terrapin
    Malaclemys terrapin

    b. Carapace scutes are smooth, with no ridges; head with orange or yellow stripes........................... 24

24. a. One to nine yellow stripes reach the eye............. 25

    b. A postorbital crescent mark prevents stripes from reaching the eye 27

25. a. A red or orange backward J-shaped postorbital mark... ....Texas Map Turtle
    Graptemys versa

    b. A square, rectangularly elongate, or oval postorbital mark 26

26. a. An oval postorbital mark, five to nine light lines reach the eye. . . . . .Sabine Map Turtle
      Graptemys sabinensis

   b. A square or rectangularly elongate postorbital mark, one to three light lines reach the eye . . . .
      . . . . Ouachita Map Turtle
      Graptemys ouachitensis

27. a. The chin has a transverse cream-colored bar . . . .
      . . . . Cagle's Map Turtle
      Graptemys caglei

   b. The chin has three dots at symphysis of jaw . . . .
      . . . . False Map Turtle
      Graptemys pseudogeographica

28. a. The upper jaw has medial notch and cusps 29
   b. The upper jaw lacks medial notch and cusps. 30

29. a. The second costal of the carapace has vertical stripes branched to form a Y-shaped figure . . . .
      . . . . Florida Red-bellied Cooter
      Pseudemys nelsoni

   b. The second costal of the carapace has five or six concentric whorls with dark centers . . . . Texas River Cooter
      Pseudemys texana

30. a. The second costal of the carapace has four distinct whorl-like blotches of concentric black and yellow rings
      . . . . Rio Grande Cooter
      Pseudemys gorzugi

   b. The second costal of the carapace has either posteriorly open C-shaped mark or a vertical bar. . . . . . .River Cooter
      Pseudemys concinna

SYSTEMATIC ACCOUNTS

Class: Chelonia

Members of the class Chelonia, or turtles, were formerly considered to be an order within the class Reptilia. The turtles are now recognized as being distinct from the Reptilia, a name that is now restricted to the lizards, snakes, amphisbaenians, and the tuatara. Chelonians are united by the possession of a bony shell that encloses the pectoral and pelvic girdles. In most species, the head, neck, and limbs can be withdrawn into the shell for protection. The oldest turtle fossils date back to the Triassic period, and the two modern orders of turtles—the Cryptodira and the Pleurodira—date back to the Jurassic and Cretaceous, respectively. The Cryptodira make up the bulk of the world's turtle species and are found throughout the northern hemisphere with recent radiations into the southern hemisphere; the Pleurodira are confined primarily to the continents of the southern hemisphere. The Chelonia is a small class containing 327 species worldwide arranged into 14 families; 58 species in 7 families occur naturally in North America north of Mexico. Texas is home to 30 native and 1 introduced species of turtle, also representing 7 families.

ORDER CRYPTODIRA

The Cryptodira include those turtles capable of withdrawing their heads into their shells by pulling them directly backward. The Cryptodira appeared in the fossil record during the late Jurassic period and are distributed primarily across the northern hemisphere, with more recent radiations into the southern hemisphere. Approximately 75% of the world's turtle species are members of the Cryptodira, including members of 11 of the world's 14 families of living turtles. All turtle species native to North America are members of this group.

FAMILY: CHELYDRIDAE

The Chelydridae are large aquatic turtles that occur primarily in North America, with a secondary radiation into Central and South America. They are predaceous species with large, powerful jaws. Because they have only limited ability to withdraw their heads and limbs into their shells, they rely primarily on these powerful jaws for self-defense. Owing to their willingness to defend themselves by biting, they are often described as aggressive or bad tempered. Their shells are rough, keeled, and serrated along their rear margin. The Chelydridae is a small family with only six species recognized globally, four of which occur north of Mexico. Two of these species occur in Texas.

Snapping Turtle
Chelydra serpentina
(Linnaeus, 1758)

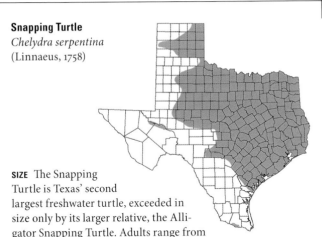

SIZE The Snapping
Turtle is Texas' second
largest freshwater turtle, exceeded in
size only by its larger relative, the Alligator Snapping Turtle. Adults range from
20 to 47 cm (8–18.5 in.) in length and in mass
from 4 to 16 kg (9–35 lb.), with exceptional wild specimens massing 34 kg (75 lb.) and an exceptional captive specimen massing
39 kg (86 lb.). Texas specimens average far smaller than do specimens from the northern part of the species' range, where the
exceptionally large specimens originated.

DESCRIPTION The carapace ranges in color from tan, olive, or dark
brown to almost black. It is usually covered with algae and (or)

Chelydra serpentina, Houston Co., Texas. Photo by Toby J. Hibbitts.

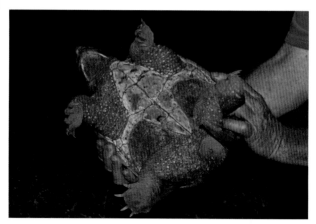

Chelydra serpentina, plastron, Marion Co., Texas.

Chelydra serpentina, hatchling, McCreary Co., Kentucky.

mud. There are three rows of weak keels running the length of the carapace, more prominent in juveniles than adults. The plastron is yellow to tan, small, and cross-shaped. The tail is as long as the carapace and armored with large dorsal scutes arranged into a saw-toothed keel. The head is large, tapering anteriorly into a slightly hooked beak. Tubercles are present on the throat and neck. The 2–3.2 cm (0.8–1.3 in.) young are much darker than are adults, black or nearly black in color, with scattered light flecks particularly on the plastron and marginal scutes.

SIMILAR SPECIES The Snapping Turtle can only be confused with its larger relative the Alligator Snapping Turtle (*Macrochelys temminckii*). The Alligator Snapping Turtle has a much more prominently hooked beak, larger and more prominent keels on the carapace, and an extra row of scutes between the marginals and the costals. Juveniles may be confused with mud and musk turtles, particularly by lay persons who view any aquatic turtle that bites as a snapping turtle, but other species have smooth shells and short tails.

DISTRIBUTION The Snapping Turtle ranges across the eastern two-thirds of the United States into southern Canada, from the foothills of the Rocky Mountains to the Atlantic Ocean. In Texas it occurs in the following river drainages: Mississippi (Canadian and Red rivers), Sabine, Neches, Trinity, Brazos, and Colorado. There are scattered records in the Nueces drainage, notably near the Gulf of Mexico, and on the Edwards Plateau along the Frio River. There is one record in the Lower Rio Grande Valley, and a few records along the Pecos River in the Trans Pecos.

NATURAL HISTORY The Snapping Turtle prefers slow-moving to stagnant, permanent bodies of freshwater with mud bottoms and abundant vegetation—such as slow rivers, streams, ox-

Chelydra serpentina, basking, Rusk Co., Wisconsin.

bows, lakes, and ponds. It will enter brackish water. The species is highly aquatic and (at least in Texas) is rarely seen basking. It is, however, frequently encountered on land as it travels from pond to pond, particularly when females are searching for nesting sites or during periods of drought when turtles may travel in search of standing water after their home pond has dried up.

The species is omnivorous, feeding upon invertebrates, carrion, fish, birds, small mammals, and (occasionally) aquatic plants. It primarily forages along the bottom of a body of water. Adults are preyed upon only by humans and alligators, but juveniles are subject to predation by a variety of mid-sized predators, including large fish, wading birds, and mammals such as raccoons. Nests are also preyed upon by crows and raccoons.

REPRODUCTION Breeding may take place from April to November with a peak in June. From 25 to 83 spherical eggs are laid 10–18 cm (3.9–7 in.) deep in a cavity. The nest may be in mud, loose soil, or rotten logs and may be hidden under logs, stumps, or roots. The eggs are 29 mm (1.1 in.) in diameter and take 9–18 weeks to hatch. In northern regions, hatchlings may overwinter in their nests, but this behavior is unlikely in most of Texas. Females may also retain sperm, allowing them to lay eggs in a season without breeding.

COMMENTS AND CONSERVATION The Snapping Turtle is one of four species of Texas turtles that may be sold in Texas provided that take of these turtles occurs on private lands or waters. Although some of these captured turtles may enter the pet trade, the vast majority of them are harvested for their meat, particularly for the international trade that supplies turtle meat to markets in China and Southeast Asia.

Alligator Snapping Turtle
Macrochelys temminckii
(Harless, 1835)

SIZE The Alligator Snapping Turtle is the largest freshwater turtle in the United States and one of the largest in the world. Adults range from 35 to 80 cm (13.8–31.5 in.) in length and in mass from 16 to 68 kg (35–150 lb.), with a record-size captive animal recorded with a mass of 143.6 kg (316 lb.). Males are significantly larger than females.

DESCRIPTION The knobby carapace is prominently keeled with three serrated ridges—a central keel along the vertebral scutes and two lateral ridges along the costal scutes. An extra row of small scutes is present between the costal and marginal scutes.

Macrochelys temminckii, old adult, Liberty Co., Texas.

Macrochelys temminckii, young adult, Tyler Co., Texas.

The rear margin of the carapace is serrated. The carapace is dark brown in most individuals but ranges from gray to black and may be covered in algae. The plastron is small, cross-shaped, and lighter in color than the carapace. The head is huge, with a prominently hooked beak and powerful jaws. The eyes are quite small. The head is typically the same color as the carapace, but in some (older?) individuals, light color may be present on the jaws and face. There are numerous branching projections of skin on the side of the head, throat, and neck. The tail is long and round and may be as long as the carapace. Although there is a row of enlarged scales on the dorsal surface of the tail, these do not form a prominent keel. The precloacal tail length increases with age in the male but not in the female.

SIMILAR SPECIES The Alligator Snapping Turtle can only be confused with the smaller Snapping Turtle (*Chelydra serpentina*). The Snapping Turtle has a proportionately smaller head with a less prominently hooked beak. Its tail possesses an enlarged row of dorsal scales that form into a dorsal keel. The carapace of the Snapping Turtle also lacks the extra row of scutes between the costals and marginals.

DISTRIBUTION The Alligator Snapping Turtle occurs in southeastern river drainages that feed into the Gulf of Mexico from the Gulf Hammock of Florida and southwest Georgia west to East Texas. Its range extends north through eastern Oklahoma to southeastern Kansas and up the Mississippi River valley to Iowa and southwest Kentucky. In Texas, it occurs in the following river drainages: Mississippi (Red and Sulphur rivers), Sabine, Neches, and Trinity.

NATURAL HISTORY The Alligator Snapping Turtle occurs in a wide variety of freshwater systems, including rivers, medium to large streams, oxbow lakes, sloughs, and swampy lakes and reservoirs. It is primarily nocturnal and does not leave the water to bask. Although it is only rarely seen from shore, trapping has shown that it may be surprisingly common. It is carnivorous, feeding primarily upon fish, but crayfish, mussels, snakes, smaller turtles, and small alligators may also be eaten.

The Alligator Snapping Turtle uses a unique worm-like appendage attached to the anterior third of its tongue to attract prey. This lure is pink and blood filled. The turtle rests on the bottom of a stream or pool with the mouth gaping, wiggling the pink "lure" about in a very convincing imitation of a worm. Potential prey investigates this lure and is met by the closing trap jaws of the snapping turtle.

The only predators of large adults are humans and perhaps alligators. As with most freshwater turtles, the eggs are preyed upon by crows and raccoons, while the young are preyed upon by large fish, wading birds, raccoons, and otters.

REPRODUCTION Breeding takes place from February through April. A single clutch of 15–30 round 3.8 cm (1.5 in.) eggs is laid sometime from April to June. The female does not travel far from water to nest, typically just above the normal high water level of the river, stream, or lake. The 3–4.4 cm (1.2–1.7 in.) hatchlings are black or dark brown with white patches of bead-like scales on the skin.

COMMENTS AND CONSERVATION The Alligator Snapping Turtle is considered a threatened species in Texas. Historically, it has been exploited for its meat. It is also threatened by unmonitored trotlines used in catfishing—one study found that turtle populations are inversely correlated to the number of unattended trotlines along Texas' rivers. It is unclear whether or not the impoundment of reservoirs on Texas' rivers has adversely affected this species. Because of its secretive and aquatic nature, the extent that it ranges upstream on Texas' rivers remains uncertain. Some southeastern populations in Florida and Georgia have been proposed to be distinct species.

FAMILY: EMYDIDAE

The Emydidae include the New World pond turtles that occur from Canada into South America, with a secondary radiation into Europe, North Africa, and the Middle East. One common North American species, the Pond Slider (*Trachemys scripta*), has been introduced via the pet trade throughout the world and can now be found on every continent except Antarctica. It is considered to be an invasive exotic species outside its native range. The Emydidae are a diverse group of terrestrial, semi-aquatic, and aquatic turtles classified together based primarily on skeletal and genetic features. The Emydidae include some of the most abundant and familiar turtles in North America. These turtles can commonly be seen basking on logs and rocks exposed in lakes, rivers, and other bodies of water—sometimes in large numbers. Globally, 52 species are recognized, 33 of which occur north of Mexico. Fifteen species occur naturally in Texas, with one species introduced by humans.

Cagle's Map Turtle
Graptemys caglei
Haynes and McKown, 1974

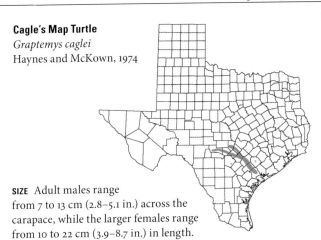

SIZE Adult males range
from 7 to 13 cm (2.8–5.1 in.) across the
carapace, while the larger females range
from 10 to 22 cm (3.9–8.7 in.) in length.
DESCRIPTION The Cagle's Map Turtle pos-
sesses a faintly reticulated to rather plain green to olive green
carapace, with black-tipped spines along the dorsal keel; juveniles are more boldly marked. The carapace is serrated along
the posterior margin. The plastron is cream colored and is often marked with scattered black flecks. The head and limbs are
boldly marked with cream-colored reticulations and stripes on
a dark gray to black ground color. The width of the stripes varies

Graptemys caglei, adult female, Guadalupe Co., Texas.

111

Graptemys caglei, adult male, Guadalupe Co., Texas.

from distinctly narrower than the dark ground color to slightly wider than the dark ground color. The head pattern varies, but usually a cream-colored transverse chin bar is present, and atop the head there is a light V-shaped mark with arms that form a crescent behind the eyes. Typically, two more crescent marks are found behind the first. The neck, tail, and legs are boldly striped in cream. As is typical in map turtles, females are larger than males and have proportionately larger heads, an adaptation that allows them to prey on mollusks.

SIMILAR SPECIES No other species of map turtle occurs in the Guadalupe River system with the Cagle's Map Turtle. No other species of map turtle in Texas possesses a cream-colored bar under the chin—instead these species have longitudinal yellow markings present in this area. Texas River Cooters (*Pseudemys texana*) lack prominent vertebral keels, have yellow head and neck stripes, and lack the crescent markings behind the eyes. Except in melanistic adults, Pond Sliders (*Trachemys scripta*) possess a bold red stripe behind the eye. Melanistic adults have uniformly black heads. This species also lacks a vertebral keel.

DISTRIBUTION The Cagle's Map Turtle occurs only in the Guadalupe River system of Texas. It ranges from Kerr County on the Edwards Plateau to Victoria County near the coast. There are reliable sight records for this species in the upper San Antonio

River of Bexar County, but these are of uncertain origin and may represent escaped captives. No extant populations are now known from the San Antonio River.

NATURAL HISTORY This species occurs throughout the Guadalupe River system but is primarily associated with stretches of river in close proximity to riffles and rapidly moving water. Above the Balcones Escarpment, it is an inhabitant of clear water, while below the escarpment it inhabits murkier waters. Adults bask on exposed rocks, cypress knees, and emergent logs.

The primary prey of Cagle's Map Turtles is various species of aquatic invertebrates, particularly arthropods such as caddis-fly larvae. The larger and proportionately larger-headed females also prey on mollusks, including snails. This particular adaptation reduces competition for food resources between the females and the smaller males and juveniles.

REPRODUCTION Courtship and copulation occur from spring to early summer. Females lay 2–3 clutches of 3–20 oval-shaped eggs per year. The 2 cm (0.8 in.) young hatch from September to November.

COMMENTS AND CONSERVATION The Cagle's Map Turtle is considered threatened by the state of Texas and has been proposed for listing at the federal level by the US Fish and Wildlife Service. Although considered threatened, it seems to be very common in some stretches of the river but not others. It is unclear why some stretches of the river harbor healthy populations while the turtles are uncommon or absent in other similar stretches.

Ouachita Map Turtle
Graptemys ouachitensis
Cagle, 1953

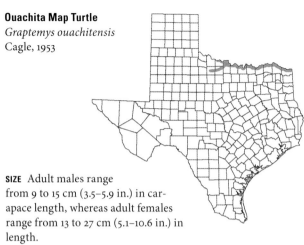

SIZE Adult males range from 9 to 15 cm (3.5–5.9 in.) in carapace length, whereas adult females range from 13 to 27 cm (5.1–10.6 in.) in length.

DESCRIPTION The Ouachita Map Turtle has a flattened, elliptical carapace with a serrated posterior edge and a prominent vertebral keel with small spine-like projections on each scute. The carapace is brown to dark green, with fine reticulations present on hatchlings and juveniles, a pattern that becomes mostly obscured in adults. The plastron is yellow to cream, pigmented in young individuals but faded or unmarked in adults. Each cos-

Graptemys ouachitensis, McCurtain Co., Oklahoma.

Graptemys ouachitensis, Bowie Co., Texas.

tal scute has yellow markings and dark blotches. The skin of the head, neck, limbs, and tail is dark olive to nearly black with yellow stripes present on all surfaces. There is a large square, rectangular, or crescent-shaped yellow spot behind the eye. One to three light stripes extend forward on the neck beneath this yellow marking and reach the eye. Three large yellow spots are present on the chin. There is no medial notch or hook on the upper jaw, and sexual dimorphism in head shape is not so pronounced in this species as it is in other map turtle species. Both males' and females' heads are relatively narrow.

SIMILAR SPECIES The sympatric False Map Turtle (*Graptemys pseudogeographica*) has a light crescent present on the head that prevents neck stripes from reaching the eye. Males and females of the False Map Turtle are also sexually dimorphic in head shape, with females possessing broadly enlarged heads. The Sabine Map Turtle (*Graptemys sabinensis*) has an oval postorbital marking, five to nine light lines that extend forward from the neck to reach the eye, and a transverse bar on the chin.

DISTRIBUTION The Ouachita Map Turtle occurs primarily in the Mississippi River drainage from central Missouri southward to the vicinity of New Orleans, Louisiana, east to central Kentucky and Tennessee, and west to central Oklahoma. In Texas, it occurs in the Mississippi drainage in the Red River. This species has been documented in the Canadian River in Oklahoma and should be searched for in this drainage in Texas.

NATURAL HISTORY The Ouachita Map Turtle occurs in large rivers and streams, lakes, and floodplain swamps. It is absent from smaller tributaries. It may be frequently seen basking on logs, rocks, and floating vegetation. It is omnivorous, feeding on insects, crustaceans, mollusks, and aquatic plants. The smaller males and juveniles of both sexes are more omnivorous than are large females, for which plants and algae make up a greater percentage of their diets.

REPRODUCTION Most reproduction occurs from May through July, with 1–3 clutches of eggs laid annually. Each clutch consists of 6–13 oval-shaped eggs. Young are 2.5–3.5 cm (1–1.4 in.) at hatching.

COMMENTS AND CONSERVATION The Ouachita Map Turtle is fairly common throughout its range in Texas. Formerly, this species was considered to be part of the False Map Turtle (*Graptemys pseudogeographica*) complex, while Texas populations now recognized as that species were considered to be a distinct species, the Mississippi Map Turtle (*Graptemys kohnii*). The Ouachita Map Turtle was also considered to be conspecific with the Sabine Map Turtle (*Graptemys sabinensis*); however, genetic data has shown the two forms to be quite distinct, with the Sabine Map Turtle actually more closely related to the Texas Map Turtle (*Graptemys versa*) and Cagle's Map Turtle (*Graptemys caglei*) than to the Ouachita Map Turtle.

Sabine Map Turtle
Graptemys sabinensis
Cagle, 1953

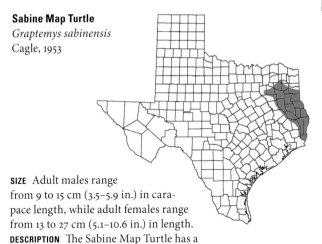

SIZE Adult males range
from 9 to 15 cm (3.5–5.9 in.) in carapace length, while adult females range
from 13 to 27 cm (5.1–10.6 in.) in length.
DESCRIPTION The Sabine Map Turtle has a
flattened, elliptical carapace with a serrated posterior edge and
a prominent vertebral keel with small spine-like projections on
each scute. The carapace is brown to dark green, with fine reticulations present on hatchlings and juveniles, a pattern that
becomes mostly obscured in adults. The plastron is yellow to
cream, pigmented in young individuals but faded or unmarked
in adults. Each costal scute has yellow markings and dark

Graptemys sabinensis, Hardin Co., Texas.

Graptemys sabinensis, Hardin Co., Texas.

blotches. The skin of the head, neck, limbs, and tail is dark olive to nearly black with yellow stripes present on all surfaces. There is a prominent oval yellow spot behind the eye. From five to nine light stripes extend from the neck forward beneath this yellow oval and contact the orbit of the eye. Transverse yellow bars are present on the chin. There is no medial notch or hook on the upper jaw, and there is little or no sexual dimorphism in head shape, with both males' and females' heads relatively narrow.

SIMILAR SPECIES The sympatric False Map Turtle (*Graptemys pseudogeographica*) has a light crescent present on the head, which prevents neck stripes from reaching the eye, and a white iris. Males and females of the False Map Turtle are also sexually dimorphic in head shape, with females possessing broadly enlarged heads. The Ouachita Map Turtle (*Graptemys ouachitensis*) has a rectangular yellow spot behind the eye, only one to three yellow lines extend forward from the neck to contact the orbit of the eye, and there are three large yellow spots on the chin.

DISTRIBUTION The Sabine Map Turtle occurs primarily in the Sabine and Neches river drainages of southwestern Louisiana and southeastern Texas.

NATURAL HISTORY The Sabine Map Turtle occurs in large rivers and streams, lakes, and floodplain swamps. It is absent from smaller tributaries. It may be frequently seen basking on logs, rocks, and floating vegetation. It is omnivorous, feeding on insects, crustaceans, mollusks, and aquatic plants. The smaller males and juveniles of both sexes are more omnivorous than are large females, for which plants make up a greater percentage of their diets.

REPRODUCTION Most reproduction occurs from May through July, with 1–3 clutches of eggs laid annually. Each clutch consists of 6–13 oval-shaped eggs. Young are 2.5–3.5 cm (1–1.4 in.) at hatching.

COMMENTS AND CONSERVATION The Sabine Map Turtle is fairly common throughout its range in Texas. Until recently this species was considered to be conspecific with the Ouachita Map Turtle (*Graptemys ouachitensis*), but genetic data has revealed it to be distinct and, in fact, more closely related to the Texas Map Turtle (*Graptemys versa*) and the Cagle's Map Turtle (*Graptemys caglei*) than it is to the Ouachita Map Turtle. Further, in the few sites in Louisiana where both the Sabine and Ouachita Map Turtle occur sympatrically, there is no evidence of hybridization. In addition, this species, together with the Ouachita Map Turtle, was once considered to be part of the False Map Turtle (*Graptemys pseudogeographica*) complex; Texas populations now recognized as the False Map Turtle were considered to be a distinct species, the Mississippi Map Turtle (*Graptemys kohnii*).

False Map Turtle
*Graptemys
pseudogeographica*
(Gray, 1831)

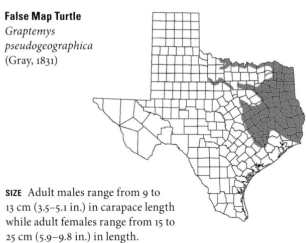

SIZE Adult males range from 9 to
13 cm (3.5–5.1 in.) in carapace length
while adult females range from 15 to
25 cm (5.9–9.8 in.) in length.

DESCRIPTION The carapace of the False Map Turtle is elliptical,
longer than wide, and with a serrated posterior edge. The middorsal keel is prominent, with short spine-like projections on
each scute. The carapace is brown to dark green, faintly marked
with reticulations in juveniles that become obscured in adults.
The plastron is yellow to cream and lacks dark pigment except
around the margins. The head, limbs, and tail are mostly dark
and are marked with yellow stripes. The boldest stripes are on
the head, with most individuals showing a distinct stripe from

Graptemys pseudogeographica, adult female, Tyler Co., Texas. Photo by Toby J. Hibbitts.

Graptemys pseudogeographica, young adult, Sabine Co., Texas.

the snout rearward between the eyes and a pair of yellow crescents behind each eye. The crescent marks behind each eye keep the neck stripes from coming in contact with the eye. In most individuals only the head stripes are prominent, with most of the stripes on the legs, neck, and tail appearing quite narrow. In some populations, the head stripes may be particularly broad and distinct. In other populations, the yellow coloration may be replaced with orange. As with most map turtles, the heads of females are larger and broader than the heads of males.

SIMILAR SPECIES In Texas, only the Ouachita Map Turtle (*Graptemys ouachitensis*) and the Sabine Map Turtle (*Graptemys sabinensis*) are found sympatrically with the False Map Turtle. These differ in having from one to nine stripes on the neck that reach the orbit of the eye and by possessing oval to square, enlarged spots behind the eye rather than a crescent marking. The Texas Map Turtle (*Graptemys versa*) also possesses neck stripes that reach the orbits of the eyes and a J-shaped marking that extends backward from the eye rather than the crescent of the False Map Turtle.

DISTRIBUTION The False Map Turtle is an inhabitant of the Mississippi River drainage of the Central United States, ranging from North Dakota, Minnesota, Wisconsin, and Indiana south to the

Graptemys pseudogeographica, upper Brazos River morphotype, Taylor Co., Texas. Photo by Michael Price.

Gulf of Mexico. In the north it occurs primarily along the major rivers of the system, including the Missouri, Ohio, and upper portions of the Mississippi River itself. In the south it also occurs in smaller streams, oxbow lakes, and swamps. In Texas it occurs in rivers of the eastern third of the state and has been found in the following drainages: Mississippi (Red and Sulphur rivers), Sabine, Neches, Trinity, and Brazos.

NATURAL HISTORY The False Map Turtle occurs in rivers, lakes, sloughs, and oxbows, often with abundant aquatic vegetation. Mud-bottomed substrates are preferred, as are abundant basking sites (primarily partially submerged trees and tree limbs). Although the species is considered omnivorous, with a range of insects, mollusks, snails, and aquatic plants included in its diet, males and females are specialized to feed on different prey items. Males and juveniles primarily eat insects and arthropods while mature females prey mostly on mollusks. Basking individuals are extremely wary and difficult to approach, diving into the water at the first distant sighting of an approaching potential predator or herpetologist. Nests, hatchlings, and juveniles face essentially the same predation threats as other aquatic turtles; adults are threatened primarily by American Alligators (*Alligator mississippiensis*) and humans.

REPRODUCTION Courtship and breeding occur primarily in the spring, with a peak in egg laying occurring in June. Two to three clutches of 8–22 eggs are laid each year. The eggs themselves are up to 41 mm (1.6 in.) long and 26 mm (1 in.) wide. Incubation takes 50–80 days, with the variation in incubation time due to temperature differences inherent in different incubation sites.

COMMENTS AND CONSERVATION False Map Turtles were once widely sold as pets. Populations have apparently declined in many areas—the causes of these declines remain unclear. Populations in the upper Brazos River system (Clear Fork of the Brazos) are apparently isolated from other Texas populations and have a distinct phenotype. These turtles are smaller and lighter in color and have orange rather than yellow markings on the head, neck, legs, and tail.

Southern populations of this species were formerly recognized as a distinct species, the Mississippi Map Turtle (*Graptemys kohnii*). To complicate matters, the Ouachita Map Turtle (*Graptemys ouachitensis*) and the Sabine Map Turtle (*Graptemys sabinensis*) were formerly considered to be part of the False Map Turtle complex.

Texas Map Turtle
Graptemys versa
Stejneger, 1925

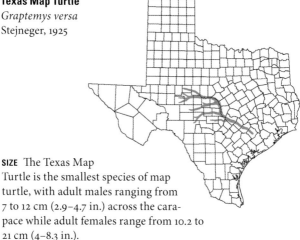

SIZE The Texas Map
Turtle is the smallest species of map
turtle, with adult males ranging from
7 to 12 cm (2.9–4.7 in.) across the carapace while adult females range from 10.2 to
21 cm (4–8.3 in.).

DESCRIPTION The Texas Map Turtle has a flattened, elliptical carapace with the anterior scutes distinctly convex, a serrated posterior margin, and a vertical keel of low, spine-like projections.
The carapace is olive to brown, with yellow reticulations on
each scute. The plastron is yellow, with pigment along the margins. The skin of the head, neck, limbs, and tail ranges from

Graptemys versa, Llano Co., Texas.

Graptemys versa, detail of head markings, Concho Co., Texas.

dark brown to black and is conspicuously marked with orange or orange-yellow stripes. A large horizontal or J-shaped line is present behind the eye and may extend rearward onto the neck. Three to six light lines extend up the neck and make contact with the orbit of the eye. The chin may be marked with one to three orange or red, black-bordered spots. The heads in both males and females are narrow but are slightly wider in older adult females.

SIMILAR SPECIES No other species of map turtle occurs sympatrically with the Texas Map Turtle. The Texas River Cooter (*Pseudemys texana*) has broad yellow stripes or spots on the head and neck and has a weakly keeled (in juveniles) or unkeeled carapace. Pond Sliders (*Trachemys scripta*) that are within the size range of the Texas Map Turtle invariably possess a broad, red postorbital stripe and have a carapace that lacks a vertebral keel. The False Map Turtle (*Graptemys pseudogeographica*) of the neighboring Brazos River drainage has a crescent-shaped postorbital stripe that prevents any of the neck stripes from contacting the orbit of the eye. The Cagle's Map Turtle (*Graptemys caglei*) of the Guadalupe River system has a cream-colored bar under the chin and stripes on the head, neck, and limbs that are whitish or whitish yellow rather than a shade of orange.

Graptemys versa, juvenile, Kimble Co., Texas.

DISTRIBUTION The Texas Map Turtle is endemic to the Colorado River system of Texas. Formerly, it was thought to occur primarily above the Balcones Escarpment in the Colorado, Concho, San Saba, and Llano rivers; however, in recent years it has been discovered to be quite abundant in the Colorado River almost to the Gulf of Mexico.

NATURAL HISTORY The Texas Map Turtle occurs in shallow rivers and streams with moderate current, numerous basking sites, and ample aquatic vegetation. Males and juveniles feed on a variety of aquatic invertebrates and algae, while large adult females feed on a wide variety of mollusks, bryozoans, sponges, and insects.

REPRODUCTION Females lay clutches of 4–9 eggs and may lay up to 4 clutches per year. Most nesting occurs from May to July.

COMMENTS AND CONSERVATION This species is quite common in Central Texas rivers. As is true with most species of Texas turtles, it is protected from commercial exploitation.

Diamond-backed Terrapin
Malaclemys terrapin
(Schaepff, 1793)

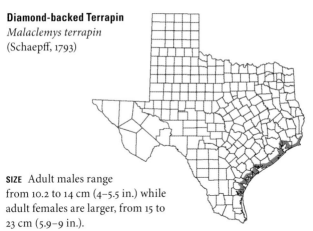

SIZE Adult males range
from 10.2 to 14 cm (4–5.5 in.) while
adult females are larger, from 15 to
23 cm (5.9–9 in.).

DESCRIPTION Diamond-backed Terrapins owe
their name to the concentric hexagonal or roughly diamond-
shaped markings on each scute. In Texas specimens the carapace is dark brown, gray, or blackish. Unlike individuals in some
populations, the central areas of the scutes are not noticeably
lighter than their edges. There is a slight vertebral keel that is
typically inconspicuous in older individuals. The rear marginal
scutes are flared upward and are slightly serrated. The plastron

Malaclemys terrapin, Galveston Co., Texas. Photograph by Toby J. Hibbitts.

Malaclemys terrapin, Galveston Co., Texas. Photograph by Toby J. Hibbitts.

is unmarked pale beige or white. The dorsal surface of the head is whitish peppered with black spots, while the legs are grayish and marked with heavier black spots. The jaws are light colored, and the eyes are black. The heads of females are enlarged, while those of males are smaller.

SIMILAR SPECIES No other species of turtle in Texas possesses a light-colored head with scattered dark markings, and most other species are unlikely to be encountered in coastal salt marsh habitats preferred by the Diamond-backed Terrapin. Pond Sliders (*Trachemys scripta*) may occasionally be found with Diamond-backed Terrapins, but these turtles have dark heads and legs marked with yellow or red stripes. Melanistic Pond Sliders have solid black or mottled heads and legs. Sea turtles have paddle-shaped front flippers.

DISTRIBUTION Diamond-backed Terrapins occur along the Atlantic and Gulf coasts from Cape Cod to Texas. In Texas, they occur from Sabine Pass to Kingsville.

NATURAL HISTORY The Diamond-backed Terrapin is an inhabitant of the brackish waters of tidal creeks, estuaries, salt marshes, lagoons, and tidal mud flats. Individuals may occasionally be observed basking on mud flats. Juveniles may be found sheltering out of water in tidal debris, such as seaweed and driftwood. Diamond-backed Terrapins are diurnal and feed on crustaceans and mollusks as adults. The larger-headed females specialize on mollusks; the diets of the small-headed males are composed predominately of crustaceans. Juveniles and hatchlings feed on a wide variety of invertebrate prey.

As with most turtles, juveniles are preyed upon by a wide variety of species, including ghost crabs, crows, shrikes, gulls, foxes, raccoons, mink, and hogs. Adults may fall prey to American Alligators (*Alligator mississippiensis*) and, in times past, humans.

REPRODUCTION Courtship and reproduction take place from April to May. Eggs are oval and pinkish white, have a leathery shell, and measure, on average, 32 mm (1.3 in.) in length. Clutch sizes range from 4 to 18 eggs, and eggs take from 9 to 15 weeks to incubate. Hatchlings range from 2.5 to 3.4 cm (1–1.3 in.) in total length. Females reach sexual maturity in 6–7 years, while males may reach sexual maturity in 3–4 years.

COMMENTS AND CONSERVATION The closest relatives to the Diamond-backed Terrapin are the map turtles of the genus *Graptemys*. Terrapins are common nowhere in Texas. Their flesh is succulent, and their populations suffered in years past due to market hunting. Today, coastal development and crab trapping are considered their biggest threats. Coastal development alters estuaries and destroys nesting sites. Turtles may become trapped in submerged crab traps and drown. Studies have shown that simple alterations of the funnels on crab traps with a 4.5 × 1.0 cm rectangle can effectively exclude turtles while not diminishing size or numbers of crabs caught.

River Cooter
Pseudemys concinna
(LeConte, 1830)

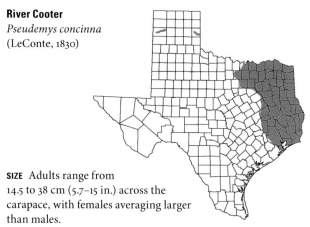

SIZE Adults range from
14.5 to 38 cm (5.7–15 in.) across the
carapace, with females averaging larger
than males.

DESCRIPTION The somewhat flattened cara-
pace is slightly serrated posteriorly and is often indented at the
bridge. The carapace is unkeeled in adults and weakly keeled
in hatchlings and juveniles. It is typically a dark olive green
in color, with lighter-colored, narrow vertical bars across each
scute. Some specimens may show a backward-facing, light-
colored C marking along the dorsal rear margin of the second
costal scute (this marking is more characteristic of populations

Pseudemys concinna, adult female, Tyler Co., Texas.

Pseudemys concinna, close-up of head, Marion Co., Texas.

Pseudemys concinna, San Jacinto Co., Texas.

east of Texas). Occasional specimens may be melanistic. Dark markings are present on the underside of the marginals. The plastron may be orange or yellow with dark pigment along the seams. An X pattern is often present anteriorly. The skin of the head, neck, legs, and tail ranges from olive to brown, with several wide yellow stripes on the underside of the neck and numerous thin, indistinct stripes on the sides and top of the head,

Pseudemys concinna, hatchling, Tyler Co., Texas.

legs, and tail. The central chin stripe forks posteriorly, forming a rear-facing Y-shaped marking. A shallow medial notch is present on the upper jaw and is not bordered by tooth-like cusps.

SIMILAR SPECIES The range of the River Cooter does not overlap with that of other species of *Pseudemys* in Texas. The Texas River Cooter (*Pseudemys texana*) possesses a notched upper jaw with tooth-like cusps bordering the notch. It is also more distinctly striped on the head and neck. The Rio Grande Cooter (*Pseudemys gorzugi*) lacks the medial notch in the upper jaw altogether, possesses a bold wide stripe behind each eye, and has four distinct whorl-like blotches of concentric black and yellow rings on the second costal scute. The Pond Slider (*Trachemys scripta*) typically has a broad, red postorbital stripe and arrow-shaped marking on the top of the head and vertical yellow stripes on the thighs. It also has a carapace that is proportionately wider than that of the River Cooter.

DISTRIBUTION The River Cooter ranges across the southeastern United States, from Texas, Oklahoma, and Kansas eastward to Virginia and the Carolinas on the Atlantic Coast. It is mostly absent from the Florida peninsula. In Texas it occurs in the following river drainages: Mississippi (Canadian, Red, and Sulfur rivers), Sabine, Neches, and Trinity.

NATURAL HISTORY The River Cooter occurs in a wide variety of streams, swamps, and lakes and is most common in situations with ample aquatic vegetation. Adults are primarily herbivorous and only rarely feed on mollusks and carrion. Hatchlings and juveniles feed on aquatic arthropods. River Cooters are primarily diurnal and frequently bask on logs when not feeding. Adults are preyed upon primarily by alligators, and hatchlings fall prey to wading birds, snakes, raccoons, and rats. Nests fall prey to crows, raccoons, skunks, opossums, and feral hogs.

REPRODUCTION Most courtship and mating occur in the spring with nesting taking place from May through July. Two clutches of 19–20 eggs are laid each year. Hatchlings emerge from August to September. Outside Texas, in northern portions of their range, hatchlings may overwinter in their nests.

COMMENTS AND CONSERVATION As with most species of turtles in Texas, the River Cooter is protected from commercial trade— both the pet trade and trade in turtle meat. These turtles may still be occasionally killed for their meat in some parts of southeast Texas. Highway mortality may be a significant cause of death in some areas.

Recent studies have suggested that species delineation in the River Cooter complex (including the Texas and Rio Grande cooters) may be oversplit, with too many species recognized, and that populations assigned to this species and the Florida Cooter complex (*Pseudemys floridana*) continue to be confused. Much research is still needed to address these issues.

Rio Grande Cooter
Pseudemys gorzugi
Ward, 1984

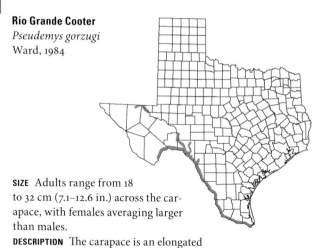

SIZE Adults range from 18 to 32 cm (7.1–12.6 in.) across the carapace, with females averaging larger than males.

DESCRIPTION The carapace is an elongated oval, flattened and with a slight vertebral keel and a serrated posterior margin. The dorsal surfaces of the carapace are primarily dark green to black, with blotches of alternating yellowish and black. The second costal scute possesses four distinct blotches with concentric black and yellow rings. The margins of the carapace, particularly the undersides of the marginals, are often red or reddish. The plastron ranges from red to yel-

Pseudemys gorzugi, adult, Kinney Co., Texas.

Pseudemys gorzugi, adult, Kinney Co., Texas.

Pseudemys gorzugi, melanistic adult, Kinney Co., Texas.

low with darker pigment present along the anterior edges of the seams. The intensity of the colored ventral pigment may fade with age. The skin is dark brown, olive, to nearly black, with pale yellow stripes present on the head, neck, legs, and tail. The yellow coloration may be replaced with red on the feet and tail in brightly marked individuals. An oval postorbital blotch is present on the side of the head, with a bold temporal stripe curving

Pseudemys gorzugi, hatchling, Val Verde Co., Texas.

dorsally over that blotch. A wide, pale yellow stripe runs down the middle of the head and neck. Another wide stripe extends forward on the sides of the neck to the angle of the jaw, where it forks, with one branch above the jaw and another below. Some older individuals may become increasingly melanistic, with the stripes on the head, neck, limbs, and tail becoming obscured. Very few individuals will lose all traces of pattern, however. The upper jaws lack a medial notch and tooth-like cusps. Males possess elongated toenails on their forelimbs, which are used in courtship.

SIMILAR SPECIES Pond Sliders (*Trachemys scripta*) typically have a distinct, red, postorbital stripe and a broader, less-elongated carapace. Melanistic individuals of Pond Sliders frequently show all black skin on the head, neck, legs, and tail, whereas melanistic Rio Grande Cooters typically show traces of pattern. The Mexican Plateau Slider (*Trachemys gaigeae*) has a large orange blotch behind the eye, extensive pigment on the center of the plastron, and a flattened green carapace with a reticulated pattern.

DISTRIBUTION The Rio Grande Cooter is endemic to the Rio Grande drainage, ranging from the Pecos River in New Mexico south to its confluence with the Rio Grande south into the Lower Rio Grande Valley nearly to the Gulf of Mexico. It occurs in the Rio Grande and its tributaries, most notably the Devils River and various spring-fed streams.

NATURAL HISTORY The Rio Grande Cooter is most common in clear-water spring runs with ample aquatic vegetation. In such situations, it may be extremely abundant. It also occurs in muddy waters of impoundments, irrigation canals, and the Rio Grande itself. It is herbivorous, feeding on aquatic vegetation.

REPRODUCTION Very little is known of the reproductive habits of this species. Presumably, its habits are similar to those of other species of cooter (*Pseudemys* spp.) that occur in Texas.

COMMENTS AND CONSERVATION Like most species of turtle in Texas, the Rio Grande Cooter is now protected from commercialization. Following its description as a distinct species in the 1980s, populations of this species in the vicinity of Del Rio were severely overcollected for the pet trade. Populations at some of these locations are much reduced even decades after these collections. It is absent from portions of the Pecos below Red Bluff Reservoir and north of Terrell County due to reduced stream flow and high levels of salinity.

Texas River Cooter
Pseudemys texana
Baur, 1893

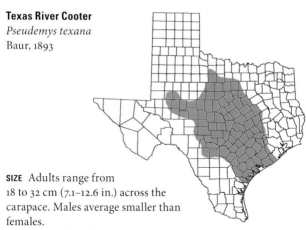

SIZE Adults range from
18 to 32 cm (7.1–12.6 in.) across the
carapace. Males average smaller than
females.

DESCRIPTION The olive to olive-brown carapace is oval, flattened, and with a serrated posterior margin. The carapace is weakly keeled in hatchlings and juveniles and unkeeled in adults. The carapace is marked with yellow lines or bars that alternate with areas of darker pigment, forming concentric whorls with dark centers. The second costal scute is marked with five or six such whorls. Some individuals may become increasingly mottled with age, obscuring the underlying

Pseudemys texana, adult, Bell Co., Texas. Photo by Toby J. Hibbitts.

Pseudemys texana, adult, Llano Co., Texas.

Pseudemys texana, reddish adult, Bosque Co., Texas.

pattern on the carapace. The plastron is yellow with darker pigment along the seams that fades with age. The skin of the head, neck, limbs, and tail ranges from dark green to nearly black and is marked with white or yellow stripes. The head markings in this species are variable and usually are broken into a series of smaller spots and dashes rather than arranged in complete

Pseudemys texana, juvenile, McLennan Co., Texas.

stripes. A postorbital stripe and vertical bar behind the angle of the jaw are often present, and the lateral head stripes curve above the vertical bar. The upper jaw is notched medially, and this notch is bordered by tooth-like cusps.

SIMILAR SPECIES The introduced Florida Red-bellied Cooter (*Pseudemys nelsoni*) has a much more highly domed carapace marked with broad, reddish, vertical bars and a head pattern consisting of a few complete stripes on a black background. The River Cooter (*Pseudemys concinna*) and the Rio Grande Cooter (*Pseudemys gorzugi*) lack the medial notch bordered by cusps on the upper jaw. Pond Sliders (*Trachemys scripta*) typically have a broad, red postorbital stripe and have rounded rather than a flat lower jaw. Texas Map Turtles (*Graptemys versa*) and Cagle's Map Turtles (*Graptemys caglei*) have a prominent dorsal keel on their carapace.

DISTRIBUTION The Texas River Cooter is endemic to Central Texas, occurring in the following river drainages: Brazos, Colorado, Guadalupe, and Nueces. In the Nueces River system it is largely confined to the eastern portion of the drainage in the Frio and Sabinal rivers and is apparently absent from the Nueces River itself.

NATURAL HISTORY The Texas River Cooter is primarily diurnal, alternating periods of foraging under the water's surface with periods of basking on logs and rocks. Adults feed primarily on aquatic vegetation; juveniles also feed upon invertebrates such as crayfish and snails. It occurs in rivers, streams, and reservoirs impounded on them and is most common at sites with abundant aquatic vegetation. Although not typically an inhabitant of ponds and stock tanks, it may be present in ponds that are located in close proximity to rivers and streams. In the water, adults are largely immune to predation but may fall prey to American Alligators (*Alligator mississippiensis*) in the lower reaches of the river drainages where alligators are present. On land, adults may face predation threats from raccoons. Hatchlings are preyed upon by fish, American Bullfrogs (*Lithobates catesbeianus*), snakes, wading birds, and mammals; nest predators include crows, raccoons, opossums, and skunks.

REPRODUCTION Courtship and breeding occur in the spring, with most nests laid in May and June. Two to four clutches of 4–19 eggs are laid per year. The eggshells have a finely granulated surface. Incubation is temperature dependent and ranges from 80 to 150 days. Males mature in 3–4 years while females may take 6 or more years to reach sexual maturity.

COMMENTS AND CONSERVATION The Texas River Cooter is among the most common turtles in the rivers of central Texas. Noticeable phenotypic variation exists between populations in different river systems, as well as between populations above and below the Balcones Escarpment in the same river system. Recent studies have suggested that the River Cooter complex (*Pseudemys concinna* complex), including the Texas River Cooter, may be oversplit and that populations assigned to this complex in some areas may be confused with populations belonging to the Florida Cooter complex (*Pseudemys floridana* complex). Much work remains to be done in order to clarify these situations.

Florida Red-bellied Cooter
Pseudemys nelsoni
Carr, 1938
Introduced

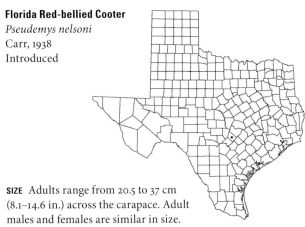

SIZE Adults range from 20.5 to 37 cm (8.1–14.6 in.) across the carapace. Adult males and females are similar in size.

DESCRIPTION The Florida Red-bellied Cooter has a distinctly high-domed carapace, an adaptation for surviving predation attempts by American Alligators (*Alligator mississippiensis*). The high-domed carapace is black or dark brown, typically with a wide vertical band on each of the costal scutes, with the band on the second costal being most prominent. In many individuals, this vertical band is a dark reddish color. The plastron is unmarked and ranges from yellowish to reddish in

Pseudemys nelsoni, male, Monroe Co., Florida.

Pseudemys nelsoni, female, Miami-Dade Co., Florida.

color, with most individuals being strongly tinted with orange, red, or coral. The upper jaw is notched, and the notch is flanked by a strong cusp. The skin of the head, neck, limbs, and tail is black. The head and neck are marked with a few slender, yellow stripes, and an arrow is present that points to the snout. Hatchlings are more colorfully marked than adults, and older adults may become melanistic with age. Adult males develop long nails on their forelimbs that they use to court females.

SIMILAR SPECIES The Texas River Cooter (*Pseudemys texana*) has a distinctly lower dome on the carapace and lacks the prefrontal arrow on the head; also, the costal scutes are not marked with broad vertical stripes. Melanistic Pond Sliders (*Trachemys scripta*) also have a lower-domed carapace and lack a notch and cusp on the upper jaw.

DISTRIBUTION The Florida Red-bellied Cooter is native to the Florida peninsula north to southeastern Georgia and the Apalachicola region of the Florida Panhandle. A small population has been introduced and become established at Spring Lake in San Marcos.

NATURAL HISTORY The habitat of the Florida Red-bellied Cooter is primarily ponds, lakes, sloughs, and marshes, preferably those with ample aquatic vegetation. It is a confirmed basker, preferring to sun itself on logs or floating mats of vegetation. Adults are primarily herbivorous, feeding on a wide range of aquatic plants. Hatchlings and juveniles have a more diverse diet and prey upon aquatic insects and arthropods as well as plants. As with other water turtles, adults are largely immune to predation except from the largest alligators and humans, while hatchlings and juveniles fall prey to a vast array of aquatic predators, including wading birds, osprey, mink, otter, water snakes, snapping turtles, and large fish.

REPRODUCTION Courtship and breeding occur from October through March. Courtship is elaborate, with the male positioning himself above the female in the water and stroking her with his enlarged forelimb claws until she either rejects or accepts his advances. Most nesting takes place in June through August, and 6–31 eggs are laid. The eggs are elliptical and average 36.5 mm (1.4 in.) in length.

COMMENTS AND CONSERVATION The Florida Red-bellied Cooter is an introduced species that is not native to Texas. Given the extent of the hatchling turtle trade in the 1960s and 1970s, it is surprising that Texas does not harbor more populations of introduced turtle species. Further introductions of this species into Texas waters are discouraged.

Painted Turtle
Chrysemys picta
(Schneider, 1783)

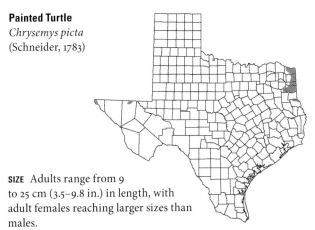

SIZE Adults range from 9 to 25 cm (3.5–9.8 in.) in length, with adult females reaching larger sizes than males.

DESCRIPTION The Painted Turtle has a low-domed or flattened oval carapace with an unserrated posterior margin. In western Texas populations, the carapace is green, olive, or olive black in coloration. It is smooth and unkeeled, with a faint net-like pattern. Red bars or crescents may be present on the marginal scutes. The margins of the carapace are smooth and may be somewhat flared. The plastron is boldly colored with irregular dark markings on a bright to pale red background.

Chrysemys picta, adult, Socorro Co., New Mexico. Photo by Toby J. Hibbitts.

Chrysemys picta, McCurtain Co., Oklahoma.

The head, neck, legs, and tail are dark green to black and are marked with yellow, reddish-yellow, or red stripes, with reddish color more likely present on the neck rather than on the head or legs. In eastern Texas populations, the scutes typically are black or dark brown and outlined in tan, yellow, or reddish color. A prominent red or reddish-yellow middorsal stripe runs down the center of the carapace. The plastron is yellow and mostly unmarked by dark pigment, with at most one or two small dark spots. The skin of the head, neck, legs, and tail is dark, ranging from a dark olive to nearly black. The head is striped with yellow. As the stripes of the head extend onto the neck, they become reddish in color. The stripes on the legs and tail are yellow. Males develop elongated forelimb claws which are used in courtship. The upper jaw is notched.

SIMILAR SPECIES Cooters (*Pseudemys* spp.) are much larger and have a higher-domed carapace on which the posterior edge is serrated and which possesses a weak median keel. Pond Sliders (*Trachemys scripta*) are greenish, possess a bright red postorbital stripe, and have higher-domed carapaces with weak medial keels and serrated margins.

DISTRIBUTION The Painted Turtle ranges from Nova Scotia to British Columbia and Washington south to Kansas and Louisiana. Isolated populations exist in the Rio Grande and Pecos rivers of New Mexico. The southern extent of these populations barely enters extreme West Texas. Rio Grande populations in El Paso County appear to have been extirpated, leaving only a small population in Culberson County. The isolated record for Wilbarger County along the Red River is outside this turtle's range and may represent a released captive. In the eastern portion of

Chrysemys picta, adult male, Missoula Co., Montana.

Chrysemys picta, adult male, Missoula Co., Montana.

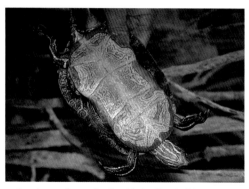

Chrysemys picta, plastron, Socorro Co., New Mexico. Photo by Toby J. Hibbitts.

Chrysemys picta, hatchling, Wood Co., Wisconsin.

the state, populations barely enter Texas in the Mississippi (Red River and Caddo Lake) and Sabine River (Toledo Bend Reservoir) drainages.

NATURAL HISTORY The Painted Turtle is the most widespread turtle in North America, and correspondingly inhabits a wide variety of bodies of water, including slow-moving rivers, streams, lakes, ponds, ditches, marshes, and prairie potholes. Water bodies with soft bottoms, ample aquatic vegetation, and exposed logs for basking hold the densest populations, although rock-bottomed lakes may also be inhabited. This species can occur in extremely dense populations in preferred habitat—with shorelines and floating mats of vegetation literally crowded with basking turtles on cool mornings when turtles seek the warmth of the sun prior to beginning their daily activities.

Painted Turtles are omnivorous, feeding on algae, vascular plants, invertebrates such as earthworms, leeches, slugs, insect larvae, and crustaceans as well as carrion, including dead fish and tadpoles. Young turtles are almost exclusively carnivorous, whereas adults are omnivores with the bulk of their diets made up of plant matter. In turn, adult Painted Turtles are preyed upon by raccoons and birds of prey, including eagles and osprey. Hatchlings face predation by a wider range of potential predators, including rats, snakes, large fish, and American Bullfrogs (*Lithobates catesbeianus*).

REPRODUCTION Courtship and breeding occur from March to June, with nesting from May through July. Females lay 1–3 clutches of 2–20 oval eggs per year. The eggs are 28–35 mm (1.1–1.4 in.) in length by 16–23 mm (0.6–0.9 in.) in diameter. The hatchlings are 2–3 cm (0.8–1.2 in.) in length with a slightly keeled carapace. Sexual maturity is attained with size, and age at maturity ranges from 2 to 5 years for males and 4 to 8 years for females.

COMMENTS AND CONSERVATION In West Texas, the Painted Turtle can be reliably encountered at only a single spring-fed pond in Culberson County. This population should be protected if this species is to be maintained as part of Texas' turtle fauna. Populations formerly present along the Rio Grande in El Paso County have apparently been extirpated due to loss of river flow and subsequent drying of riverside marshes. Although they barely occur in eastern Texas, the populations present are apparently stable and thriving in Toledo Bend Reservoir and Caddo Lake. Painted Turtles were formerly a staple in the pet trade, but closure to the take of native turtles throughout most this species' range has eliminated this threat.

Mexican Plateau Slider
Trachemys gaigeae
(Hartweg, 1939)

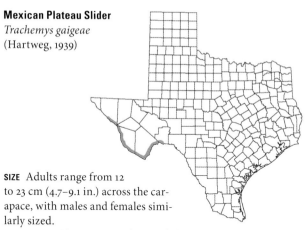

SIZE Adults range from 12 to 23 cm (4.7–9.1 in.) across the carapace, with males and females similarly sized.

DESCRIPTION The Mexican Plateau Slider has a weakly keeled, low-domed or slightly flattened carapace with a slightly serrated posterior margin. The carapace is olive to olive brown in coloration, with an intricate pattern of orange lines or reticulations. Dark spots are present on the underside of each marginal scute. The plastron is white, orange, or light green with dark pigments present along the transverse seams between scutes. The upper jaw is medially notched. The skin of the head, neck, legs, and tail is light green, olive, or brownish. The most prominent mark is a large oval spot behind the eye that is orange to red in color and bordered by black. This mark does not

Trachemys gaigeae, Sierra Co., New Mexico. Photo by Toby J. Hibbitts.

Trachemys gaigeae, old adult, Presidio Co., Texas.

touch the orbit. Lateral stripes on the head and neck are otherwise yellowish and broken into small spots or ovals. A yellow median stripe is present on the chin. The forelegs are marked with horizontal yellow stripes, and the hind limbs are marked with vertical yellow stripes. Although melanism is not as common in this species as it is in its close relative, the Pond Slider (*Trachemys scripta*), older individuals may become increasingly suffused with dark pigment, ultimately resulting in a virtually unmarked dark gray or black turtle. Males of this species lack the long claws on the forelimbs characteristic of most of their close relatives.

SIMILAR SPECIES No similar turtle occurs sympatrically with the Mexican Plateau Slider in Texas. The Painted Turtle (*Chrysemys picta*) occurs in the Rio Grande of New Mexico alongside the Mexican Plateau Slider. It is similar in size and shape but lacks the black-bordered spot behind the eye and typically has a bright red plastron where the two species co-occur. The closely related Pond Slider (*Trachemys scripta*) has been introduced into ponds in southern Brewster County and occurs naturally in the Lower Canyons of the Rio Grande in Terrell County. It has elongated yellow, orange, or red postorbital stripes that touch the orbit. Rio Grande Cooters (*Pseudemys gorzugi*) are larger and lack the orange, black-bordered spot behind the eye. Males of

Trachemys gaigeae, Presidio Co., Texas.

all three of these species possess elongated forelimb claws used in courtship.

DISTRIBUTION The Mexican Plateau Slider occurs primarily in the Rio Grande drainage of the United States and Mexico, with outlying populations occurring in Mexico's Rio Nazas drainage. In the United States this turtle occurs in two disjunct populations, the first in the Rio Grande of central New Mexico and the second in the Rio Grande of Texas' Big Bend Region, from Culberson to Terrell counties. It also occurs in the Rio Conchos of Mexico.

NATURAL HISTORY The Mexican Plateau Slider occurs primarily in slow-moving portions of the river. It may also occupy cattle tanks, canals, and sloughs adjacent to the river. It typically basks on emergent rocks in the river itself and may also utilize gravel bars and the muddy banks of the river for basking if other suitable sites are not available. It is omnivorous, with adults primarily subsisting on vegetable matter while young feed preferentially on aquatic invertebrates.

REPRODUCTION Courtship and breeding occur from March through July, with the bulk of the nesting taking place in June and July. Up to 3 clutches of 4–23 eggs are laid each year. Incubation takes from 60 to 75 days, depending upon incubation temperature. Courtship in this species involves males approaching and chasing females from behind, a behavior unlike that of the closely related Pond Slider, in which males approach females from the front.

COMMENTS AND CONSERVATION Mexican Plateau Sliders are threatened by decreasing stream flow in the Rio Grande. The now isolated populations in central New Mexico and Texas' Big Bend region may have historically been contiguous before water diversion for agriculture in the region between El Paso and Las Cruces.

The Mexican Plateau Slider is also threatened by genetic intermingling with its close relative, the Pond Slider (*Trachemys scripta*). Pond Sliders will hybridize with Mexican Plateau Sliders when the two species come into contact. Historically, rapids in the Lower Canyons of the Rio Grande prevented Pond Sliders from coming into contact with Mexican Plateau Sliders. However, in recent years reductions in flow have allowed populations of Pond Sliders to bypass those rapids and to hybridize with Mexican Plateau Sliders in Terrell County. In addition, Pond Sliders have long been a staple of the pet trade, and they have intentionally been released into the habitat of the Mexican Plateau Slider. This problem is particularly evident in central New Mexico. Although less of a problem in the Big Bend region of Texas, a population of Pond Sliders has been present near Lajitas in southern Brewster County for at least 20 years, and hybrids have been detected in the Rio Grande in this area as well.

Pond Slider
Trachemys scripta
(Schoepff, 1792)

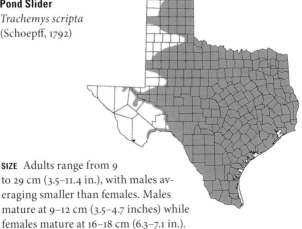

SIZE Adults range from 9 to 29 cm (3.5–11.4 in.), with males averaging smaller than females. Males mature at 9–12 cm (3.5–4.7 inches) while females mature at 16–18 cm (6.3–7.1 in.).

DESCRIPTION Most Pond Sliders that occur in Texas possess a distinct red stripe behind the eye and are often referred to as "Red-eared Sliders." The skin is green, olive, or brownish, with conspicuous head markings in all but melanistic individuals. A wide red or orange black-bordered stripe extends rearward from the eye forming an elongated oval blotch. Wide yellow stripes are present on the sides of the face and chin extending

Trachemys scripta, adult female, Chambers Co., Texas.

Trachemys scripta, adult female, Aransas Co., Texas.

Trachemys scripta, detail of head, Karnes Co., Texas.

rearward onto the neck, and fine yellow stripes are also present on the head and neck. An arrow-shaped mark on top of the head is formed by a stripe across the snout and the supratemporal stripes. The limbs are marked with fine yellow stripes as well, and the rump is marked with well-defined vertical stripes. Many older specimens, particularly males, become melanistic with age, with the colorful light stripes and green ground color becoming increasingly replaced with black and dark gray pigment, both on the skin and the shell. The carapace is roughly

Trachemys scripta, melanistic male, Collin Co., Texas.

oval and weakly keeled. The rear border of the carapace is weakly serrated. In all but melanistic individuals, the carapace is green, olive, or brown marked with yellow or orange lines on the costal and vertebral scutes. The pattern varies from simple bars and stripes to reticulations and ocelli (eye-like spots). The plastron is predominately yellow and typically has a single dark spot on each scute. The upper jaw is medially notched. Mature males possess long toenails used for courtship.

SIMILAR SPECIES Throughout most of its range in Texas, the Pond Slider is the most abundant turtle, particularly in the still waters of lakes, ponds, and other impoundments. It may be confused with the cooters (*Pseudemys* spp.), which lack the red postocular stripe, have deeper shells, reach larger sizes as adults, and possess an upper jaw with a notch that is bordered on each side by a cusp. Painted Turtles (*Chrysemys picta*) have flatter, smooth, unserrated carapaces and also lack the red postocular stripe. The Chicken Turtle (*Deirochelys reticularia*) has a long neck, more elongate carapace, and broad foreleg stripes. The Pond Slider can be distinguished from its close relative, the Mexican Plateau Slider (*Trachemys gaigeae*), by its larger size, deeper and more highly domed carapace, possession of elongated foreclaws in males, and a reddish or orange postorbital stripe rather than a single, rounded postorbital blotch.

DISTRIBUTION The Pond Slider ranges from the Pecos River drainage of New Mexico northeast to the southern terminus of Lake Michigan and east to Chesapeake Bay. It is absent from most of the Appalachian mountain chain and peninsular Florida. It also ranges south into Mexico along the Gulf Coast through Central America to Brazil. As a staple in both the pet trade and the Asian turtle meat trade, it has been widely introduced outside its native range and may be found in scattered locations from the Pacific Northwest to Southern California. Populations have also become established at various locations throughout the world, and it now occurs on every continent except Antarctica. In Texas it occurs statewide except for the upper portions of the Rio Grande in the Trans Pecos. One notable introduced population occurs in the Lajitas area in southwestern Brewster County. Although tied to rivers only in the western part of its range, in Texas it may be found in all major river drainages, absent only from the upper portions of the Rio Grande.

NATURAL HISTORY The Pond Slider prefers still waters of lakes, ponds, ditches, bayous, swamps, and oxbows. It may also be found in slow-moving sections of rivers, creeks, and streams. Areas with ample basking spots and dense aquatic vegetation are preferred. It is predominately diurnal and is among the most obvious of water turtles, spending a great deal of time basking, with numerous individuals congregating at preferred basking sites, even to the point of stacking one turtle on top of another. Of Texas' water turtles, this is the species most likely to be encountered far from water as individuals move from one pond to another, particularly after rains. It may be observed throughout the year in most of Texas. Adults are omnivorous, feeding on vegetation, aquatic invertebrates such as arthropods and mollusks, small vertebrates including fish and tadpoles, as well as upon carrion. Hatchlings and juveniles are primarily carnivorous, feeding primarily on small aquatic invertebrates. Adults are preyed upon by alligators, gar, crows, mink, raccoons, otter, coyotes, and humans. In addition to these predators, nests and young also face predation from snakes, wading birds, skunks, raccoons, ants, and fly maggots.

REPRODUCTION Courtship occurs from March to June. Males approach females from the front and stroke the female's face and legs with the elongated claws on the male's forelimbs. If his overtures are accepted, the female will allow the male to mate with her. Nesting follows mating by about one month, with most clutches laid from April to July. Females may lay up to 5 clutches per year, with clutch sizes ranging from 2 to 23 eggs per clutch. The oval-shaped eggs average 37 mm (1.5 in.) in length and take 60–80 days to incubate, depending mostly upon temperature. Hatchlings range from 2.8 to 3.3 cm (1.1–1.3 in.) and possess a bright green carapace with a distinct pattern. In northern climates, some young overwinter in their nests—a situation that is rare in Texas.

COMMENTS AND CONSERVATION The Pond Slider is extremely abundant in Texas and is almost certainly the single most numerous turtle in the state. It is one of four turtle species that may be collected commercially, both for the pet trade and for the trade in turtle meat centered in Southeast Asia. Released individuals have established populations throughout the world, and it is considered to be an invasive pest outside its native range.

Chicken Turtle
Deirochelys reticularia
(Latreille, 1801)

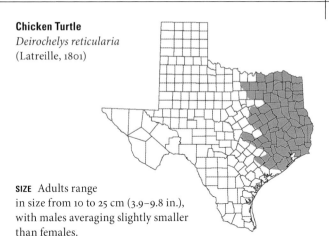

SIZE Adults range
in size from 10 to 25 cm (3.9–9.8 in.),
with males averaging slightly smaller
than females.

DESCRIPTION The Chicken Turtle's most nota-
ble feature is its extremely long head and neck, which can extend nearly as long as the animal's carapace. The dark olive
skin of the head and neck is narrowly striped in yellow, and the
underside of the neck is unpatterned. There are vertical "pinstripes" on the rump and a wide stripe on each forelimb. The
carapace is roughly oval, widest at the rear, and dorsoventrally
flattened. The rear margin of the carapace is smooth and lacks

Deirochelys reticularia, adult, Kaufman Co., Texas.

Deirochelys reticularia, Liberty Co., Texas.

the serrated margin present in most other pond turtles. The scutes of the carapace are rough with a somewhat finely wrinkled appearance. The carapace is dark greenish, olive, or brownish, with a faint net-like pattern of reticulations. The rim of the shell is yellow. The plastron is yellow and largely unmarked, although some specimens show dark markings along the margins of the scutes. Young turtles possess a slight keel.

SIMILAR SPECIES When its neck is fully extended, the long neck separates the Chicken Turtle from any other species of pond turtle in Texas. In Pond Sliders (*Trachemys scripta*), Painted Turtles (*Chrysemys picta*), and River and Texas River Cooters (*Pseudemys concinna* and *Pseudemys texana*), the first vertebral scute does not come into contact with four marginal scutes as it does in the Chicken Turtle. Pond Sliders also have vertical pinstripes on their hind limbs but lack the broad stripes on their forelimbs and have serrated rear carapace margins, unlike the Chicken Turtle.

DISTRIBUTION The Chicken Turtle inhabits the coastal plains from southeastern Virginia to Florida and west to eastern Texas. It also ranges up the Mississippi River valley to Missouri and Oklahoma. In Texas, this species has been documented from the drainages of the Mississippi (Sulphur and Red), Sabine, Neches, Trinity, Brazos, and Colorado rivers, although the turtles themselves are primarily inhabitants of swamps, oxbows, and ponds.

NATURAL HISTORY The Chicken Turtle inhabits shallow waters with dense vegetation, ranging among marshes, sloughs, lakes, ponds, swamps, and roadside ditches. Young turtles are carnivorous, and adults are omnivores, feeding on vegetation, invertebrates, tadpoles, crayfish, and carrion. In turn, the adults

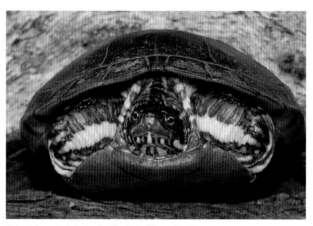

Deirochelys reticularia, detail of forelimbs, Liberty Co., Texas.

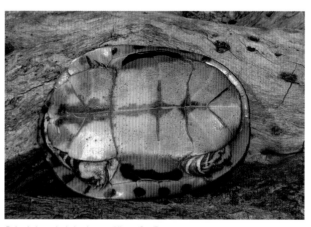

Deirochelys reticularia, plastron, Liberty Co., Texas.

are preyed upon primarily by alligators and humans, while juveniles, hatchlings, and eggs fall prey to raccoons, skunks, and wading birds.

REPRODUCTION Sexual maturity is reached by males in their second or third year when their carapace length reaches 8 cm (3.1 in.). Females reach sexual maturity 1–2 years later at lengths averaging 15 cm (5.9 in.). Courtship and reproduction may occur in fall (September through November) or spring (February through April). Several clutches of 5–15 elliptical 37 mm (1.5 in.) long eggs are laid in shallow cavities in loose soil. Those clutches laid late in the fall may overwinter in their nests and hatch in the early spring. Hatchlings range from 2.5 to 3.2 cm (1–1.3 in.) in length.

COMMENTS AND CONSERVATION The Chicken Turtle is uncommonly encountered in Texas and little is known about its abundance in the state. As an inhabitant of ponds and other ephemeral wetlands subject to drying, it may wander far afield in search of water during droughts, making it susceptible to traffic fatalities when crossing highways. The common name "Chicken Turtle" is an allusion to their palatable flesh rather than the length of their neck.

Eastern Box Turtle
Terrapene carolina
(Linnaeus, 1758)

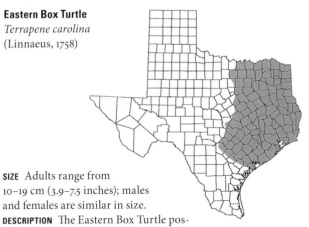

SIZE Adults range from
10–19 cm (3.9–7.5 inches); males
and females are similar in size.

DESCRIPTION The Eastern Box Turtle possesses a high-domed carapace with a weak
vertebral keel present in scutes 2–4. The rear margin is smooth
and unserrated. The carapace is tan, brown, or olive and may
be unmarked or marked with faint radiating stripes, which fade
with age. The edges of the scutes are marked with darker pigment along the seams. The plastron is dark brown or tan, patterned only with dark pigment along the seams. There is a
transverse hinge across the plastron that enables the turtle to

Terrapene carolina, adult, McCurtain Co., Oklahoma.

Terrapene carolina, detail of head, male, Marion Co., Texas.

completely close its shell with its head, legs, and tail fully protected by the bony shell. The rear portion of the plastron may
be slightly concave in adult males. The skin of the head, neck,
limbs, and tail ranges from brown to black and may be streaked
or spotted with a combination of red, orange, yellow, or white,
particularly on the head and forelimbs. Males are more colorful than are females, and some individuals may have entirely
red heads. The iris of the male is red while females have yellow
or brown irises. The upper jaw possesses a slight, downturned
beak. The feet are unwebbed, and in most Texas individuals,
three toes are present on their hind limbs.

SIMILAR SPECIES The Eastern Box Turtle may be confused with
its close relative, the Ornate Box Turtle (*Terrapene ornata*). The
Ornate Box Turtle has a more flattened carapace with a pattern of radiating yellow lines on each scute. The plastron is also
boldly marked with light and dark radiating lines. Mud Turtles
(*Kinosternon* spp.) possess two hinges on their plastrons and
cannot close their shells completely.

DISTRIBUTION The Eastern Box Turtle ranges from Central Texas,
Oklahoma, and Kansas east across the eastern United States to
Michigan and Massachusetts and south into the Florida peninsula. Disjunct populations of Eastern Box Turtles in the Mexican states of Tamaulipas, San Luis Potosí, and Veracruz and on
the Yucatan Peninsula likely represent distinct species. In Texas

it occurs throughout the eastern third of the state, mostly east of a line extending from San Antonio north to Fort Worth.

NATURAL HISTORY The Eastern Box Turtle occurs in open woodlands, grasslands, and meadows and may reach its highest densities in floodplain forests. It is primarily terrestrial but can sometimes be found wading in water or mud. It basks in the early morning or late afternoon prior to foraging and may retreat to shallow burrows during the heat of the day or during hot, dry weather. The turtle digs its own burrows under logs or vegetation. It may be particularly active after spring and summer rains. The Eastern Box Turtle is omnivorous, feeding on fruits, roots, seeds, mushrooms, insects, earthworms, small vertebrates, and carrion. While adults are largely immune to predation, hatchlings are preyed upon by snakes, birds of prey, and small mammals. The invasive Red Fire Ant (*Solenopsis invicta*) has been implicated as a predator on newly emerging hatchlings that are still in their nests. Nests may fall prey to skunks, foxes, raccoons, crows, and snakes. Eastern Box Turtles are extremely long-lived.

REPRODUCTION Male courtship seems to consist largely of males persistently following and attempting to mount receptive females. Most nests are laid from May through July. Four to five eggs are laid per clutch, and up to 5 clutches may be laid per year. Females may lay fertile eggs for several years following a single mating. Incubation is temperature dependent and ranges from 70 to 80 days. Hatchlings are soft-shelled and dully marked, typically brown or tan with an irregular light marking on each scute. Sexual maturity is reached in 5–7 years.

COMMENTS AND CONSERVATION Populations of the Eastern Box Turtle are in decline throughout Texas, primarily from habitat fragmentation and road mortality. In past years Texas populations of the Eastern Box Turtle were exploited commercially for the pet trade, with many thousands of these slowly reproducing turtles being removed from the wild. Today, Eastern Box Turtles are protected from such exploitation.

Recent genetic work suggests that Texas and neighboring populations may be distinct from populations in the eastern United States, despite apparent intergradations between these populations. If these studies are supported by more evidence, Texas populations would be elevated to specific rank and regarded as the Three-toed Box Turtle (*Terrapene triunguis*).

Ornate Box Turtle
Terrapene ornata
(Agassiz, 1857)

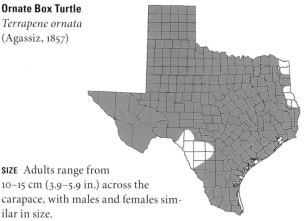

SIZE Adults range from
10–15 cm (3.9–5.9 in.) across the
carapace, with males and females similar in size.

DESCRIPTION Ornate Box Turtles have a black,
dark brown, or reddish-brown carapace that is boldly marked
with yellow or yellowish radiating lines on each scute and a yellow middorsal stripe. Eastern populations possess from 5 to
8 yellow stripes on the second costal scute, while Trans Pecos
populations possess from 8 to 14. Most individuals remain well
marked throughout life, but some older Trans Pecos specimens
may lose their patterns and become uniformly brownish or horn

Terrapene ornata, adult male, Matagorda Co., Texas.

Terrapene ornata, adult female, Presidio Co., Texas.

Terrapene ornata, adult male, Presidio Co., Texas.

colored. The carapace is domed and lacks a serrated rear margin. The plastron is dark brown with a distinct pattern of lighter radiating lines. A distinct hinge is present on the plastron that enables the shell to completely enclose the head, neck, and limbs when closed. The skin of the legs, neck, and tail is brown or olive brown marked with yellowish spots. Males and females are sexually dimorphic with regard to skin color. Males typically

Terrapene ornata, plastron, Austin Co., Texas.

have a greenish head and have bright red spots on the forelimbs, while females have brown heads and forelimbs that are spotted with pale yellow markings. Males also have a red iris; the iris of females is yellowish brown. The rear portion of the plastron is slightly concave in males. Ornate Box Turtles possess four toes on their hind feet with the inner toe capable of turning inward. Their upper jaw is slightly beaked without a central notch.

SIMILAR SPECIES The Eastern Box Turtle (*Terrapene carolina*) is never so boldly marked as the Ornate Box Turtle, has a plastron not marked in alternating dark and light radiating lines, and has a carapace that is more highly domed. Mud Turtles (*Kinosternon* spp.) have two plastral hinges and cannot close their shells completely. The Texas Tortoise (*Gopherus berlandieri*) is a plain brown turtle, has distinct concentric growth rings on each scute, and lacks hinges on the plastron altogether.

DISTRIBUTION The Ornate Box Turtle inhabits much of the south-central portion of the United States from Arizona east to Louisiana and north to Indiana, Wisconsin, and North Dakota. It also occurs in northern Sonora and Chihuahua, Mexico. In Texas, it occurs statewide.

NATURAL HISTORY The Ornate Box Turtle is most abundant on open prairies devoid of trees but also ranges into semiarid grasslands and savannahs as well as occurring in open grassy

Terrapene ornata, hatchling, Randall Co., Texas.

areas in pine forests of deep East Texas. It is diurnal and may be seen basking in the early morning or late afternoon. During the heat of the day, it seeks shelter under rocks, logs, vegetation, or in animal burrows. Summer rains may increase its activity. Although it is omnivorous, the bulk of its diet consists of insects, carrion, eggs, and small vertebrates, with only a small percentage of its diet coming from fruit and other vegetable matter. It has been documented to search cattle dung for beetles. Because of its ability to completely close its shell for protection, adults have few enemies. Adults may occasionally be accidentally trampled by livestock. Nests and hatchlings may fall prey to Gopher Snakes (*Pituophis catenifer*), hawks, ravens, crows, opossums, badgers, raccoons, cats, dogs, and coyotes. Nestlings may also be susceptible to predation by the imported Red Fire Ant (*Solenopsis invicta*) while they are emerging from their eggs.

REPRODUCTION Most reproduction occurs in spring and early summer. Females lay up to 2 clutches of 2–8 eggs per year. Incubation is temperature dependent and lasts approximately 80 days. Hatchlings are pale gray in color with a single light mark at the center of each scute. Sexual maturity is reached in 8–10 years.

COMMENTS AND CONSERVATION Ornate Box Turtles were formerly collected by the thousands for the pet trade but are now protected from commercial exploitation by TPWD regulations. Populations of Ornate Box Turtles are declining throughout most of the state, with habitat loss, alteration, and fragmentation being the primary causes of decline. Road mortality may also be a significant cause of decline, particularly in the eastern portion of the state.

FAMILY: TESTUDINIDAE

The Testudinidae includes the tortoises and is the only family of turtles in which all members are considered to be primarily terrestrial. Most tortoises are readily recognizable with their high-domed carapaces, prominent growth rings on their scutes, armored forelimbs often modified for digging, and elephantine hind limbs. Tortoises occur primarily in tropical regions of South America, Africa, and Asia, with a few species radiating into temperate regions of those continents as well as into North America and Europe. Some island species, such as the Galapagos Tortoise (*Chelonoidis elephantopus* complex) and the Aldabra Tortoise (*Aldabrachelys gigantea*), reach enormous sizes—up to 1.3 m (4.3 ft.) across the carapace and in excess of 120 kg (264 lb.). There are 57 species recognized globally, 3 of which occur north of Mexico (with a fourth species occurring in the region during Holocene times and now represented by a relict population in northern Mexico). A single species is native to modern Texas.

Texas Tortoise
Gopherus berlandieri
(Agassiz, 1857)

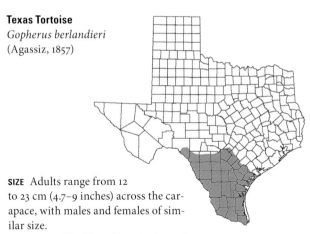

SIZE Adults range from 12 to 23 cm (4.7–9 inches) across the carapace, with males and females of similar size.

DESCRIPTION The Texas Tortoise has a short, high-domed carapace with a serrated posterior margin. Prominent growth rings are present on the scutes of both the carapace and plastron, giving each scute a rough, ridged appearance. The carapace ranges from gray to brown, with the center of each scute lighter in color. The plastron is similar in color to the carapace but lighter in hue. It is unhinged and possesses a prominent gular projection that curves upward. The posterior of the

Gopherus berlandieri, adult male, Uvalde Co., Texas.

Gopherus berlandieri, detail of head, Uvalde Co., Texas.

plastron is flat in females and concave in males. The bridge between the carapace and plastron is broad, and two axillary scutes are present. The skin of the head, neck, limbs, and tail ranges from gray to yellowish brown and is unmarked. The head is wedge shaped. Thick scales are present on the anterior surfaces of the forelimbs; the remaining skin surfaces are smooth. The forelimbs are shovel shaped and the hind legs are elephantine. The claws are gray or brown, and the toes are not webbed.

SIMILAR SPECIES No other species native to Texas is very similar to the Texas Tortoise. Box turtles (*Terrapene* spp.) possess a hinged plastron that lacks the gular projection found in the Texas Tortoise, and their scutes are not distinctly light centrally and lack prominent growth rings.

DISTRIBUTION The Texas Tortoise ranges across southern Texas south of a line from Del Rio to San Antonio southeast to Port Aransas. In Mexico, it also occurs in eastern Coahuila, northern Nuevo Leon, and throughout Tamaulipas.

NATURAL HISTORY The Texas Tortoise is an inhabitant of Tamaulipan Thornscrub habitats of southern Texas. Although it ranges into rocky areas along the margins of the Edwards Plateau, it prefers sandy, well-drained soils. It may be found active year round, although individuals in the northern parts of its range undergo dormancy in cold weather. The Texas Tortoise is di-

Gopherus berlandieri, detail of gular scutes, Frio Co., Texas.

Gopherus berlandieri, juvenile, Dimmitt Co., Texas.

urnal and may be active throughout the day in the spring and fall, while during midsummer heat it adopts a bimodal activity pattern with activity restricted to early mornings and late afternoons. It is herbivorous, feeding on grasses, annual plants, and the stems, flowers, and fruits of cacti. It may eat the droppings from other tortoises. Most of its water needs are met from the water contained in its food, limiting its need to drink. It does not excavate extensive burrows as other US species of tortoise do, instead scraping out shallow depressions under brush or cacti or taking refuge in the burrows of other animals, such as armadillos. Adults are largely immune to predation, whereas hatchlings and juveniles fall prey to a host of terrestrial predators including snakes, birds of prey, raccoons, skunks, bobcats, foxes, and coyotes. Two adult Indigo Snakes (*Drymarchon melanurus*) that we collected in Starr County were found to contain the remains of five hatchling tortoises. Nests are preyed upon by crows, raccoons, and skunks.

REPRODUCTION Courtship and mating occur in the spring. Males may engage in territorial combat when they encounter one another at this time of year, using their gular projections to tip their opponents onto their backs. When male and female meet, courtship involves face-to-face head bobbing followed by copulation. Most nesting occurs in June and July, but eggs may be laid as late as September in some years. Females lay 1–3 eggs per nest and up to 7 eggs total per season. Incubation is temperature dependent and lasts 85–115 days. The 4–5 cm (1.6–2 in.) hatchlings emerge from August through October. Sexual maturity is reached in 3–5 years.

COMMENTS AND CONSERVATION The Texas Tortoise is considered a threatened species by the TPWD and was the first species of turtle so designated in Texas. Prior to protection as a threatened species, thousands of individuals entered the pet trade annually, severely depleting some populations. Conversion of rangeland to crop production has also severely impacted some populations. Increasingly, road mortality has been implicated as a cause of decline. While respiratory tract infections have been implicated in declines among Desert Tortoises (*Gopherus agassizii*) in California, this disease has not seriously impacted Texas Tortoise populations. However, Texas populations should be closely monitored for the presence of this disease. Despite the Texas Tortoise's herbivorous diet, some ranchers still think that they feed on quail eggs and unnecessarily and illegally persecute them.

FAMILY: TRIONYCHIDAE

The softshell turtles are a highly specialized group of turtles with a flattened carapace on which the horny scutes have been replaced by a supple, leathery skin. They are highly aquatic turtles with broad, webbed feet, are strong swimmers, and are highly predaceous. Many species hunt by burying themselves in shallow sand or silt on the bottoms of bodies of water at a depth at which they can just reach the surface with their snorkel-like snouts. Here they wait in ambush for passing fish or invertebrates. They are capable of significant respiration across their moist skins as well as through the linings of their mouths and cloacae. They occur in North America, Africa, and southern and eastern Asia. Thirty species are recognized globally, three of which occur north of Mexico. Two species occur in Texas.

Smooth Softshell
Apalone mutica
(LeSueur, 1827)

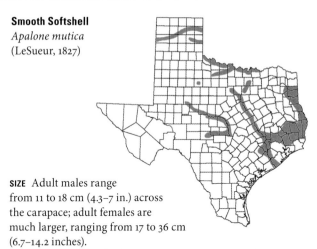

SIZE Adult males range
from 11 to 18 cm (4.3–7 in.) across
the carapace; adult females are
much larger, ranging from 17 to 36 cm
(6.7–14.2 inches).

DESCRIPTION The flat, leathery carapace is smooth, lacking spines, bumps, or small dorsal projections. In most specimens it is brownish but ranges from gray to olive. A light marginal band is present. Males and juveniles show very little dark mottling on the carapace, while adult females may be strongly mottled with darker coloration. The plastron is unmarked and lighter than the carapace. The skin of the head, neck, limbs, and tail

Apalone mutica, Montgomery Co., Texas. Photo by Toby J. Hibbitts.

177

Apalone mutica, Coleman Co., Texas.

matches the coloration of the carapace dorsally, ranging from brown to gray or olive, and is lighter ventrally, ranging from cream to gray. A dark-bordered light line extends through the eye rearward onto the neck. The feet are highly webbed and are unmarked with dark pigment. The tail in the male is very long. The mandibles are very sharp. The snout is tubular, and the nostrils lack a septal ridge.

SIMILAR SPECIES The Smooth Softshell can be confused with only its close relative, the Spiny Softshell (*Apalone spinifera*). Spiny Softshells have ridges on the internasal septum, possess spines or knobs on the anterior margin of the carapace, and have patterned forelimbs. Juvenile and young male Spiny Softshells are typically boldly patterned with light spots on the carapace.

DISTRIBUTION The Smooth Softshell occurs primarily in the Mississippi River drainage of the Central United States. In the south, it ranges from central Alabama and western Florida west to eastern New Mexico, while in the north it ranges from western Pennsylvania west to south–central North Dakota. In Texas, it has been found in scattered locations in the following river drainages: Mississippi (Canadian and Red rivers), Sabine, Neches, Trinity, Brazos, and Colorado rivers. Most Texas records are associated with the Canadian, Red, Brazos, and upper

Colorado rivers. The distribution of this species in Texas needs to be investigated in greater detail.

NATURAL HISTORY The Smooth Softshell occurs primarily in large rivers and streams with sandy bottoms. It may also occur in reservoirs on the same rivers and streams but is rarely present in smaller bodies of water. It prefers situations with moderate to fast current and is a powerful swimmer. It is a diurnal species and frequently basks on banks, logs, and rocks. During warmer weather, it may be found basking underwater in the shallows. It spends long periods of time buried in sand on river bottoms at a depth just deep enough so that the surface can be reached by the snout. It is primarily an ambush predator, feeding on invertebrates and small fish. Juveniles prefer larval insects. It is a milder-tempered species than the Spiny Softshell and less prone to lunging open-mouthed strikes. Adults may be preyed upon by American Alligators (*Alligator mississippiensis*); juveniles fall prey to fish, other turtles, snakes, and wading birds. Nests fall prey to the same host of nest predators as other aquatic turtles.

REPRODUCTION Courtship occurs in the spring, mostly in March and April. Mating occurs underwater. Nesting occurs from May through July. Several clutches of 11–33 eggs are laid high above the water on sand bars and banks exposed to the sun. The eggs are 20–24 mm (0.8–0.9 in.) in diameter and have a thick brittle shell. Incubation is temperature dependent and typically ranges from 65 to 80 days. Hatchlings are 30–45 mm (1.2–1.8 in.) across the carapace. Males reach sexual maturity in 4–5 years at sizes between 8 and 8.5 cm (3.1–3.3 in.) while females take 7–9 years to reach sexual maturity at sizes between 14 and 15 cm (5.5–5.9 in.).

COMMENTS AND CONSERVATION Although the Smooth Softshell is uncommon throughout most of Texas, it is one of four species subject to commercial harvest (primarily due to difficulty in distinguishing it from the abundant Spiny Softshell). The range of the Smooth Softshell in Texas is poorly understood, and it is absent from many locations with seemingly suitable habitat.

Spiny Softshell
Apalone spinifera
(LeSueur, 1827)

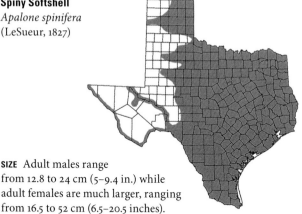

SIZE Adult males range
from 12.8 to 24 cm (5–9.4 in.) while
adult females are much larger, ranging
from 16.5 to 52 cm (6.5–20.5 inches).

DESCRIPTION The Spiny Softshell has a flat,
leathery carapace with numerous small spine-like projections
along the anterior edge. The leathery surface of the carapace
also has a sandpapery surface owing to the presence of numerous small dorsal projections. The ground color of the carapace
ranges from tan to olive, usually with a pale margin bordered
by a dark line. In juveniles and adult males the carapace may
be liberally sprinkled with light spots or dark ocelli. In larger

Apalone spinifera, adult female, Kinney Co., Texas.

Apalone spinifera, young male, Edwards Co., Texas.

adult females, the juvenile pattern is replaced by irregular dark blotches. The plastron is yellowish or whitish. The skin of the head, neck, limbs, and tail ranges from tan to olive on their dorsal surfaces and cream to gray ventrally. Two black-bordered light lines are present on the head, with one extending through the eye and the other through the angle of the jaws. These lines may be obscured in older adult females. The limbs are marked with dark spots and streaks, particularly on the webbing between the toes. The snout is tubular, and the nostrils possess a ridge on the medial surfaces of the septum. The tails of adult males are much longer than the tails of females.

SIMILAR SPECIES The Spiny Softshell can be confused with only its close relative the Smooth Softshell (*Apalone mutica*). The Smooth Softshell is typically browner, lacks spines on the anterior border of the carapace, and further lacks the ridge on the internasal septum.

DISTRIBUTION The Spiny Softshell ranges across the central United States, from Montana to Vermont in the north and from New Mexico to the Carolinas in the south. Introduced populations occur in Arizona and California. In Texas, it occurs in all major river drainages.

NATURAL HISTORY The Spiny Softshell occurs in a wide variety of aquatic habitats, ranging from the flowing waters of rivers,

Apalone spinifera, juvenile, Edwards Co., Texas.

streams, and canals to lakes, ponds, oxbows, and bayous. It prefers and is most abundant in areas with muddy or soft bottoms
but also utilizes areas with rocky substrates. It is highly aquatic,
and only egg-laying females are likely to be found more than a
few feet away from water. It is diurnal, and when not foraging it
may be seen basking on banks, logs, or rocks. In warm weather,
it may bask submerged just beneath the surface of the water in
the shallows. It is primarily an ambush predator; it hunts in areas with the water just shallow enough that it can bury itself in
mud or sand with its head exposed so that its nostrils can reach
the surface. In addition to respiring through the lungs, softshell
turtles also have a limited ability to respire through their skins
and cloacae. The diet of the Spiny Softshell is almost entirely
carnivorous, consisting of aquatic insects, crayfish, and small
fish. In turn, it faces threats of predation similar to those seen in
other aquatic turtles.

REPRODUCTION Nesting occurs from May through August. Two
clutches of 12–18 eggs are laid per year, typically in an exposed
location in full sun. The 29 mm (1.1 inch) eggs are white with
a thick, brittle shell. Incubation is temperature dependent and
usually lasts from 70 to 85 days. Hatchlings emerge from August
to October and are 30–40 mm (1.2–1.6 in.) in carapace length.

Males reach sexual maturity at 8–9 cm (3.1–3.5 in.) while females reach sexual maturity at 18–20 cm (7.1–7.8 in.).

COMMENTS AND CONSERVATION The Spiny Softshell is one of the most abundant turtle species in Texas and is one of four species that may be harvested for commercial purposes. Although a few of these turtles may enter the pet trade, most are destined for meat markets in Southeast Asia. Spiny Softshells are often hooked on fishing lines baited with live bait. Removing hooks from a defensive turtle's mouth is a difficult and somewhat perilous endeavor, and most anglers simply cut the line above the hook, leaving the hook embedded in the turtle's mouth. Most such turtles will ultimately starve.

FAMILY: KINOSTERNIDAE

The Kinosternidae includes 25 species of small- to medium-sized semiaquatic turtles ranging from Canada to South America. All members of this family are capable of secreting a foul-smelling musk from glands near the bridge between the plastron and carapace, giving rise to the common name "musk turtle" for many species. Many species inhabit stagnant, muddy waters and may burrow into mud as these waters dry, giving rise to the common name "mud turtles" used for other species in this family. The Kinosternidae are omnivorous, forage by walking on the bottoms of bodies of water, and may include carrion as a significant portion of their diets. Ten species occur north of Mexico, five of which occur in Texas.

Yellow Mud Turtle
Kinosternon flavescens
(Agassiz, 1857)

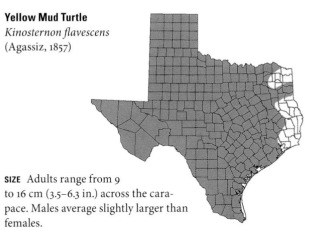

SIZE Adults range from 9 to 16 cm (3.5–6.3 in.) across the carapace. Males average slightly larger than females.

DESCRIPTION The olive or olive-brown carapace is oval and somewhat flattened. It lacks a vertebral keel and the posterior margins are not serrated. The first vertebral scute is in contact with the second marginal, and the ninth and tenth marginal scutes are elevated above the remaining marginals. The plastron is short and narrow, with 11 scutes and two well-developed hinges. The pectoral scutes are triangular in shape. The plastron ranges from yellow to brown, with dark seams

Kinosternon flavescens, Brewster Co., Texas.

Kinosternon flavescens, Ector Co., Texas. Photo by Toby J. Hibbitts.

Kinosternon flavescens, detail of head, Frio Co., Texas.

around the margins of each scute. The dorsal surfaces of the head, neck, limbs, and tail are olive or grayish brown, while the ventral and lateral surfaces are unmarked and yellow. In males, the inner surface of the hind legs is roughened and the tail is thick and tipped with a spine.

SIMILAR SPECIES All other mud turtles have the ninth marginal scute the same height or only slightly higher than the eighth marginal. In the Rough-footed Mud Turtle (*Kinosternon* *hirtipes*), the pectoral scutes meet in a point or are only narrowly in contact whereas the pectoral scutes are broadly in contact in the Yellow Mud Turtle. Musk turtles (*Sternotherus* spp.) have a much smaller, narrower plastron with only a single, poorly developed hinge.

DISTRIBUTION The Yellow Mud Turtle ranges across much of the south–central United States from Nebraska south through Texas into northern Mexico. Isolated populations exist in Iowa, Illinois, and Missouri. Yellow Mud Turtles have been documented from the Mexican states of Durango, Chihuahua, Coahuila, Nuevo Leon, and Tamaulipas. In Texas, the species occurs throughout the western two-thirds of the state.

NATURAL HISTORY The Yellow Mud Turtle is an inhabitant of slow-moving and standing water, including streams, canals, ditches, cattle tanks, and lakes. It prefers sites with soft bottoms of either sand or mud. It is primarily diurnal, but in the heat of the summer may shift its activity patterns to include some nocturnal activity. It occasionally basks on logs, rocks, or floating vegetation. Individuals may frequently be found far from water, especially after spring or summer thunderstorms or when waterholes dry. During drought, most bury into the muddy bottoms of their waterholes and enter into a period of dormancy known as aestivation. Yellow Mud Turtles are omnivorous but feed mostly on animal matter, including snails, crayfish, aquatic insects, fish, amphibians, and carrion. Vegetation found in their stomachs may be only secondarily ingested along with their prey. In turn, they are preyed upon by fish, water snakes, hawks, and larger turtles. Their hatchlings and nests fall prey to nest predators such as crows, rodents, raccoons, and skunks.

REPRODUCTION Most mating occurs in the spring, and eggs are laid from May to June. Females lay up to 2 clutches of 1–9 eggs per year. Incubation time is temperature dependent and ranges from 95 to 115 days. Hatchlings emerge from August to October, are 1.7–2.4 cm (0.7–0.9 in.) in length, and have a yellow and black plastron.

COMMENTS AND CONSERVATION Yellow Mud Turtles are common throughout most of their range, and large numbers of individuals may inhabit a single pond. Due to the murky nature of the waters they inhabit, they frequently go unnoticed. Like most species of turtle in Texas, the Yellow Mud Turtle is protected from commercial exploitation.

187

Rough-footed Mud Turtle
Kinosternon hirtipes
(Wagler, 1830)

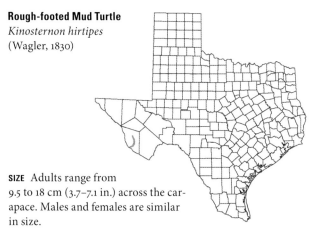

SIZE Adults range from
9.5 to 18 cm (3.7–7.1 in.) across the carapace. Males and females are similar
in size.

DESCRIPTION The olive-brown carapace is oval
in shape, with a well-developed medial keel and two weakly defined lateral ones. The rear margin of the carapace is unserrated. The first vertebral scute is in contact with the second marginal, and the tenth marginal scute is elevated above the ninth marginal. The edges of the scutes along the seams between them are darkened. The plastron is short and narrow, with 11 scutes and two well-developed hinges. The pectoral scutes are triangular in

Kinosternon hirtipes, Presidio Co., Texas.

Kinosternon hirtipes, Durango, Mexico. Photo by Toby J. Hibbitts.

shape. The plastron is tan to brown and, like the carapace, has darkened scute margins along the seams. The skin of the head, neck, legs, and tail ranges from tan to dark brown or black. The head and neck are marked with a reticulated pattern of small, dark spots and streaks. Three barbels are present on the chin.

SIMILAR SPECIES In the United States, only the Yellow Mud Turtle (*Kinosternon flavescens*) is similar and sympatric with the Rough-footed Mud Turtle. It differs in having a flatter, unkeeled carapace with the ninth marginal scute higher than the eighth, pectoral scutes that meet at a point or are only narrowly in contact, and a yellow throat and neck.

DISTRIBUTION In the United States, the Rough-footed Mud Turtle occurs only in the Rio Grande drainage's Alamito Creek in Presidio County, where it is restricted to a series of artificial impoundments (stock tanks) along the now-dry watercourse of Alamito Creek. In Mexico, it occurs primarily in Chihuahua, Durango, western Coahuila, and Zacatecas.

NATURAL HISTORY Throughout most of this turtle's range, it occurs in slow-moving pools of rivers and streams in mesquite grasslands and lower mountain slopes. It also takes advantage of artificial impoundments, including cattle tanks. It is highly aquatic and rarely visible from the surface. These turtles are highly carnivorous, feeding on crustaceans, snails, aquatic insects, worms, fish, and amphibians. Little is known about its daily activity patterns, but like other mud turtles, it may be active both diurnally and nocturnally.

REPRODUCTION Courtship and breeding may occur from May to September, with 2 clutches of 1–7 eggs laid per year. The 28 mm (1.1 in.) eggs incubate in 196–201 days, depending on temperature. Hatchlings are 20–27 mm (0.8–1.1 in.).

COMMENTS AND CONSERVATION The Rough-footed Mud Turtle is considered threatened by the TPWD. Today this turtle is restricted to a few spring-fed stock tanks in the otherwise dry Alamito Creek watershed. Prior to the 1880s, Alamito Creek was a meandering, marshy stream dotted with beaver ponds. Overgrazing and drought led to extensive streamside erosion and channelization of the streambed, and today the stream is dry and rocky for most of the year, leaving these turtles restricted to scattered isolated ponds.

Eastern Mud Turtle
Kinosternon subrubrum
(Lacépède, 1788)

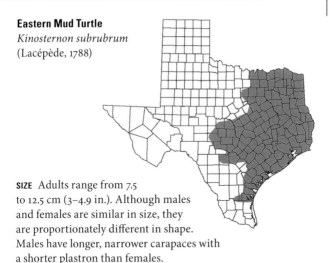

SIZE Adults range from 7.5 to 12.5 cm (3–4.9 in.). Although males and females are similar in size, they are proportionately different in shape. Males have longer, narrower carapaces with a shorter plastron than females.

DESCRIPTION The Eastern Mud Turtle is a small, dark turtle with a distinctly oval and rounded carapace. The carapace is unmarked olive or dark brown. No medial keel is present, and the rear margins are not serrated. The first vertebral scute is not in contact with the second marginal scute, and all of the marginal scutes are similar in height. The plastron is unmarked yellow

Kinosternon subrubrum, Oklahoma.

191

Kinosternon subrubrum, hatchling, Austin Co., Texas. Photo by Toby J. Hibbitts.

Kinosternon subrubrum, plastron of hatchling, Austin Co., Texas. Photo by Toby J. Hibbitts.

to brown. It is short and narrow, with 11 scutes and two well-developed hinges. The pectoral scutes are triangular. The skin is olive or brown. Most Texas individuals have yellow spotting and a pair of light stripes on the face and neck. Fleshy barbels are present on the head and neck. Males have a blunt spine on the tip of the tail, with a notch on the rear of the plastron that is reduced or missing on the female.

SIMILAR SPECIES The Stinkpot (*Sternotherus odoratus*) has a similar pattern—a pair of stripes—on the face and neck, but it has a keeled carapace and small, narrow plastron with a single hinge rather than the paired plastral hinges of the Eastern Mud Turtle. Yellow Mud Turtles (*Kinosternon flavescens*) have an unmarked face with a yellow throat, a carapace that is lower and broader, and a ninth marginal scute that is much higher than the eighth.

DISTRIBUTION The Eastern Mud Turtle ranges from extreme southern New York south to the Florida peninsula west to Central Texas and up the Mississippi River valley to Indiana and Illinois. In Texas, it occurs in roughly the eastern half of the state in the following river drainages: Mississippi (Red and Sulphur rivers), Sabine, Neches, Trinity, Brazos, Colorado, Guadalupe, and Nueces.

NATURAL HISTORY The Eastern Mud Turtle occurs in slow-moving bodies of water with soft bottoms and abundant aquatic vegetation, including streams, lakes, marshes, ditches, oxbow lakes, bayous, lagoons, and coastal marshes in both fresh and brackish water. These turtles are diurnal, with activity peaks early and late in the day. It may be terrestrial for long periods of time and is not often seen basking. It is omnivorous, feeding on vegetation, aquatic insects, crayfish, snails, amphibians and their larvae, and carrion. When confronted by a potential predator, it secretes a noxious musk. As with most turtle species, nests are preyed upon by a wide variety of predators, including king snakes, opossums, weasels, skunks, raccoons, foxes, and crows. Juveniles are preyed upon by snakes, predatory fish such as gar, crows, and wading birds. Adults are preyed upon by alligators and birds of prey.

REPRODUCTION Nesting occurs from May to June; 1–3 clutches of 2–4 eggs are laid each year. The elongated elliptical eggs are 22–32 mm (0.9–1.3 in.) in length, and incubation is completed in 90–100 days. Hatchlings are 2.3–2.5 cm (0.9–1 in.) in length.

COMMENTS AND CONSERVATION Eastern Mud Turtles are locally common to abundant throughout their range. They occur in the greatest population densities in the Coastal Prairies and Marshes region of Texas.

Razor-backed Musk Turtle
Sternotherus carinatus
(Gray, 1855)

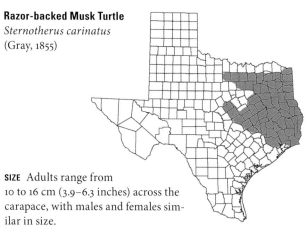

SIZE Adults range from
10 to 16 cm (3.9–6.3 inches) across the
carapace, with males and females similar in size.

DESCRIPTION The aptly named Razor-backed
Musk Turtle features an orange- to brown-streaked carapace
with a bold, prominent middorsal keel. The dark brown spots or
streaks radiate from the posterior corner of each scute. Furthermore, the posterior scute margins may also be darkened. These
markings may become reduced or absent with age, producing
a uniformly brown shell. The rear margins of the carapace are
slightly serrated, and the vertebral scutes overlap. The plastron
is yellow with no dark pigment; it is small with 10 scutes and a
single, indistinct hinge. No gular scute is present. The skin of
the head, neck, legs, and tail is light with scattered dark spots

Sternotherus carinatus, Tyler Co., Texas.

Sternotherus carinatus, Hardin Co., Texas.

and may be brown, olive, gray, or pinkish. The jaws are tan with dark streaks. Two fleshy barbels are present on the chin. The head of these turtles is relatively large in comparison with the size of their carapace.

SIMILAR SPECIES Stinkpots (*Sternotherus odoratus*) possess a less distinctly keeled carapace that is usually darker in coloration. They also normally have two light lines on the sides of the head and have barbels present on both the chin and throat. Mud turtles (*Kinosternon* spp.) have large plastrons with two distinct hinges.

DISTRIBUTION The Razor-backed Musk Turtle occurs primarily in the lower Mississippi Valley region, ranging from eastern Texas and southeastern Oklahoma through southern Arkansas and Louisiana to western Mississippi. In Texas, it occurs primarily in the following river drainages: Mississippi (Red and Sulfur rivers), Sabine, Neches, Trinity, and Brazos.

NATURAL HISTORY The Razor-backed Musk Turtle inhabits slow-moving waters of swamps, rivers, streams, and reservoirs impounded on rivers and streams. It prefers areas with soft bottoms and abundant aquatic vegetation. It is active mostly diurnally, primarily in mornings and afternoons, retreating to cool waters during the heat of the day. Razor-backed Musk Turtles may be observed basking more often than other species of mud and musk turtles, climbing high onto rocks, logs, and over-

Sternotherus carinatus, juvenile, captive specimen.

hanging branches that emerge from the water. It is omnivorous, feeding on a wide variety of aquatic insects, crustaceans, mollusks, amphibians, fish, and carrion as well as on aquatic vegetation. It hunts by walking along the bottom of a body of water in search of food. As with all mud and musk turtles, this species is capable of expelling musk, but unlike other species (notably, the Stinkpot), it rarely does so. Its nests and hatchlings face similar predation challenges as other aquatic turtles. Predators of adult Razor-backed Musk Turtles are not well documented but may include American Alligators (*Alligator mississippiensis*), Alligator Snapping Turtles, raccoons, and other mid-sized predators.

REPRODUCTION Nesting occurs in May and June, with 1–2 clutches averaging 5 eggs each laid in soil or rotting logs. The incubation period ranges from 110 to 120 days and is temperature dependent. Hatchlings are 23–31 mm (0.9–1.2 in.) and may have three keels on the carapace rather than the single middorsal keel seen in adults. Females reach sexual maturity in 4–5 years with a carapace length of approximately 10 cm (3.9 in.), while males mature in 5–6 years with a carapace length between 10 and 12 cm (3.9–4.7 in.).

COMMENTS AND CONSERVATION Razor-backed Musk Turtles are often quite abundant in favorable habitat. Because of their preference for carrion, they are often caught on fishing lines. Owing to the difficulty removing hooks from the mouths of these turtles, most lines are cut, leaving the hook in the turtle's mouth, which usually results in a slow death by starvation.

Stinkpot
Sternotherus odoratus
(Latreille, 1802)

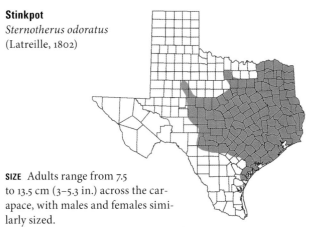

SIZE Adults range from 7.5 to 13.5 cm (3–5.3 in.) across the carapace, with males and females similarly sized.

DESCRIPTION The dark carapace is highly arched with either an indistinct or no vertebral keel in adults (the vertebral keel is present in hatchlings and juveniles). The rear margin of the carapace is unserrated and the vertebral scutes do not overlap. In color, the carapace ranges from olive to dark brown or black. Juveniles and young adults have darker streaks present on each scute while older adults are unmarked. The plastron is small with 11 scutes and a single indistinct hinge. The pectoral scutes are rectangular. The plastron is yellow to brown with no darker markings. The skin of the head, neck, legs, and tail is dark gray to black. A pair of white to yellow

Sternotherus odoratus, McCurtain Co., Oklahoma.

Sternotherus odoratus, Edwards Co., Texas.

Sternotherus odoratus, Runnels Co., Texas.

stripes prominently marks the sides of the head and neck. The stripes extend from the nostrils rearward, with one stripe passing above the eye and the other extending diagonally below the eye to the point of the jaw and beyond. These stripes are present in all but the oldest individuals. The jaws are tan with dark streaks. Barbels are present on both the chin and neck. Males possess much larger heads than do females.

SIMILAR SPECIES Populations of the Eastern Mud Turtle (*Kinosternon subrubrum*) that occur in Texas possess a similar pattern of light lines on the side of the face but possess a much larger plastron with two distinct hinges. Razor-backed Musk Turtles (*Sternotherus carinatus*) possess a distinctly keeled carapace that is lighter in color with overlapping vertebral scutes, and the head in this species possesses scattered dark spots on a light background.

DISTRIBUTION The Stinkpot ranges across most of the eastern half of the United States, from Texas, Oklahoma, and Kansas northeast to Wisconsin, southern Michigan, and southern Manitoba east to Maine. It also occurs south along the Atlantic seaboard throughout the Florida peninsula. In Texas, it is associated with the following river drainages: Mississippi (Red and Sulphur rivers), Sabine, Neches, Trinity, Brazos, Colorado, Guadalupe, and Nueces.

NATURAL HISTORY The Stinkpot is most abundant in slow-moving bodies of water with muddy bottoms, including lakes, swamps, rivers, streams, sloughs, canals, bayous, and oxbows. It may also be found in rock-bottomed streams in Central Texas and in the highlands of the Ouachita and Ozark plateaus of Oklahoma, Arkansas, and Missouri. It may be active both during daylight and at night. Although it is not a frequent basker, some may oc-

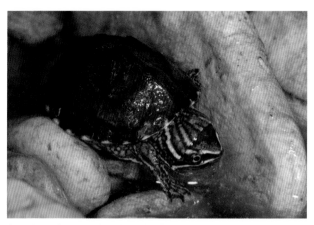

Sternotherus odoratus, hatchling, Kimble Co., Texas.

casionally climb high into branches to bask. The carapace of many individuals may be covered with large growths of algae, which serves to help camouflage individuals resting on the bottom of streams. Although all mud and musk turtles are capable of exuding foul-smelling musk to repel potential predators, none do so as readily as the Stinkpot. Stinkpots are omnivorous, feeding on a wide variety of insects, earthworms, snails, crabs, crayfish, tadpoles, fish, carrion, and algae. They actively forage by patrolling the bottoms of bodies of water for food. In turn, they are preyed upon by a wide variety of predators. Adults face predation by alligators, snapping turtles, raccoons, and birds of prey, while hatchlings are preyed upon by fish, American Bullfrogs (*Lithobates catesbeianus*), and snakes. As with most turtles, their nests are preyed upon by snakes, skunks, raccoons, and crows.

REPRODUCTION Courtship and mating take place underwater. Nesting takes place from February through July. Females lay up to 4 clutches of 4–5 eggs per year, often in communal nests with other females. Eggs may be deposited in soil or in rotted logs. The eggs are small, averaging 27 mm in size (1.1 in.), and incubation takes from 68 to 85 days. The tiny hatchlings are 19–25 mm (0.7–1 in.) across the carapace. Males mature in 4–7 years at approximately 6.5 cm (2.6 in.) in length, while females reach sexual maturity in 5–8 years at lengths between 6.5 and 8.5 cm (2.6–3.3 in.).

COMMENTS AND CONSERVATION Stinkpots are rather common throughout much of their range, although due to their preference for dark waters and infrequent basking they are often overlooked. Because of their preference for carrion, they are often hooked by anglers. Due to the difficulty removing hooks from the mouths of these turtles, most lines are cut, leaving the hook in the turtle's mouth, which usually results in a slow death by starvation.

FAMILY: CHELONIIDAE

The Cheloniidae includes six species of hard-shelled sea turtles that inhabit primarily tropical, subtropical, and warm temperate marine waters. Their forelimbs are modified into long flippers, and they gracefully swim by "flying" through the water. All sea turtles mate at sea, and females clumsily haul themselves ashore to lay eggs on sandy beaches. Hatchling sea turtles face severe predation upon hatching as they emerge from nests and struggle into the surf, with near 99% mortality occurring in the first year of life. Six species occur in the world's oceans, five of which reach waters north of Mexico. Four of these species occur in the Gulf of Mexico off the Texas coast.

Loggerhead Sea Turtle
Caretta caretta
(Linnaeus, 1758)

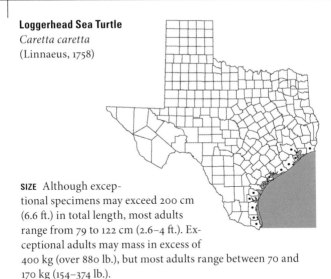

SIZE Although exceptional specimens may exceed 200 cm (6.6 ft.) in total length, most adults range from 79 to 122 cm (2.6–4 ft.). Exceptional adults may mass in excess of 400 kg (over 880 lb.), but most adults range between 70 and 170 kg (154–374 lb.).

DESCRIPTION The carapace is typically reddish brown, tinged with olive in some individuals. Some scutes may have yellow borders. A vertebral keel that becomes smoother with age is present. The posterior rim of the carapace is serrated. The carapace possesses

Caretta caretta, adult, Kleberg Co., Texas. Photo courtesy National Park Service-Padre Island National Seashore (NPS-PAIS).

Caretta caretta, hatchling, Kleberg Co., Texas. Photo courtesy NPS-PAIS.

5 or more pairs of costals and 11–15 marginals. There are three poreless inframarginals. The bridge between the carapace and plastron is cream to yellowish, as is the unmarked plastron itself. Hatchlings and juveniles possess longitudinal ridges on the plastron that disappear with age. As its name implies, the head is large, broad, and rounded at the front. The snout is short, with two pairs of prefrontal scales between the eyes. The jaws are yellow, and the lower jaw is smooth. Males have broader heads with more yellow pigment than do females.

SIMILAR SPECIES Loggerhead Sea Turtles can be confused with only other similar sea turtles. The Kemp's Ridley Sea Turtle (*Lepidochelys kempii*) is smaller, gray, and has four inframarginals on the bridge, each of which possesses pores. The Green Sea Turtle (*Chelonia mydas*) is typically more greenish, has a smaller head, and has only one pair of prefrontal scales between the eyes. Hawksbill Sea Turtles (*Eretmochelys imbricata*) are smaller, have a distinctly hooked beak, and are more colorful.

DISTRIBUTION The Loggerhead Sea Turtle is an inhabitant of warm temperate and tropical waters throughout the world's oceans. It occurs throughout the Caribbean and has been encountered in coastal waters all along the Texas Coast. Records exist from 12 Texas counties (Jefferson, Harris, Galveston, Brazoria, Calhoun, Aransas, Nueces, Kleberg, Kennedy, Willacy, and Cameron).

NATURAL HISTORY This is a marine species that occurs from coastal waters out to 240 km (149 mi.) into the open sea. In the Gulf Stream currents, it can usually be found in the cooler water of the western boundaries of the current. It may enter bays, lagoons, salt marshes, and the mouths of large rivers. Subadults and adults are free swimming, but hatchlings float in or near mats of sargassum. The species is omnivorous, feeding upon sponges, mollusks, crustaceans, sea urchins, and plants.

REPRODUCTION Mating occurs in deep offshore waters. Nesting has been recorded from April to August, with most Texas nesting occurring April to July. It nests at night on sloping beaches. Individual females lay several clutches of 105–125 eggs several times during the nesting season at intervals ranging from 10 days to 6 weeks. A female may nest every 2–3 years. The eggs take 55–60 days to hatch. Sexual maturity is reached in 15–20 years.

COMMENTS AND CONSERVATION The Loggerhead Sea Turtle is the most common sea turtle in Texas waters. Globally, it is considered threatened, and it is so listed by both the United States and Texas governments. Beach development has reduced or destroyed many nesting areas and has increased populations of nest predators such as raccoons by providing them with shelter and supplementary food supplies found in human garbage. Although shrimp boats are now required to equip their nets with Turtle Excluder Devices (TEDs), many sea turtles likely still die in shrimping nets. Emerging hatchlings may also be attracted to artificial lights, causing them to move toward lights and away from the sea, where they may be killed on highways or desiccate and die away from the water.

Green Sea Turtle
Chelonia mydas
(Linnaeus, 1758)

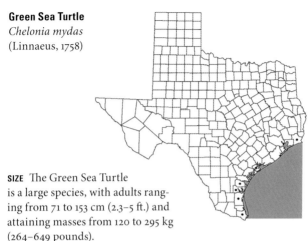

SIZE The Green Sea Turtle
is a large species, with adults ranging from 71 to 153 cm (2.3–5 ft.) and
attaining masses from 120 to 295 kg
(264–649 pounds).

DESCRIPTION The Green Sea Turtle has a broad, oval-shaped, unkeeled carapace (except in hatchling and very young turtles,
which do possess a keel). In color, the carapace ranges from
pale, olive, or dark green to dark brown. Some specimens may
be lightly mottled or have radiating stripes on the costal scutes.
The first costal scute does not touch the nuchal scute. There are
four scutes on the bridge connecting the carapace to the plas-

Chelonia mydas, adult, Kleberg Co., Texas. Photo courtesy NPS-PAIS.

Chelonia mydas, hatchling, Kleberg Co., Texas. Photo courtesy NPS-PAIS.

tron. The plastron is white or yellowish. The head possesses a pair of prefrontal scales between the eyes. The male's tail extends past the edge of the carapace and is tipped with a horny nail. The flippers have a single claw present.

SIMILAR SPECIES The Green Sea Turtle can be confused with only other sea turtles. It can be differentiated from the Loggerhead Sea Turtle (*Caretta caretta*) by examining the carapace—in the Loggerhead, the first costal scute is in contact with the nuchal. The Kemp's Ridley Sea Turtle (*Lepidochelys kempii*) is smaller, and the first costal scute is also in contact with the nuchal. The smaller Hawksbill Sea Turtle (*Eretmochelys imbricata*) is more colorful, has two pairs of prefrontal scales, and has larger scutes on the carapace that may overlap.

DISTRIBUTION The Green Sea Turtle occurs in warm temperate and tropical oceans throughout the world, including the Gulf of Mexico. In Texas, it has been recorded from only six counties (Jefferson, Calhoun, Nueces, Kleberg, Kennedy, and Cameron). Although Green Sea Turtles are sighted from time to time in Texas' coastal waters, most of these records represent dead turtles that have washed up on Texas beaches.

NATURAL HISTORY The preferred habitat of the Green Sea Turtle is shallow waters with abundant aquatic plants. It may be seen in deeper waters as it migrates from one feeding ground to another or from feeding grounds to nesting beaches. Young turtles spend their first year floating in mats of seaweed in areas far away from the feeding grounds of the adults. In their second year, they return to the shallow feeding areas utilized by the adults.

The diet of this species varies with age. Young and juvenile turtles feed upon worms, crustaceans, and aquatic insects. Adults are the only species of Texas sea turtle that is herbivorous, feeding primarily on aquatic vegetation.

REPRODUCTION Green Sea Turtles nest every 2–4 years; 100–120 golf-ball-sized eggs are laid at night in urn-shaped nests 1–8 times per nesting season. The eggs take approximately 60 days to hatch. Green Sea Turtles take 20–30 years to reach sexual maturity.

COMMENTS AND CONSERVATION Although this species is considered to be endangered globally, and is on the United States' and Texas' threatened species lists, adults and eggs are still commercially harvested for food in many parts of the world. The skin is also used for leather products, and the body fats and oils are used as a base for cosmetics and cooking oils.

Hawksbill Sea Turtle

Eretmochelys imbricata
(Linnaeus, 1766)

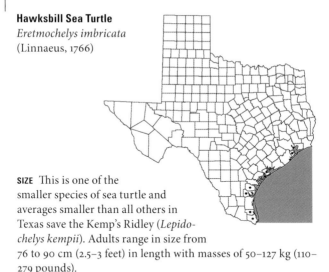

SIZE This is one of the smaller species of sea turtle and averages smaller than all others in Texas save the Kemp's Ridley (*Lepidochelys kempii*). Adults range in size from 76 to 90 cm (2.5–3 feet) in length with masses of 50–127 kg (110–279 pounds).

DESCRIPTION The Hawksbill Sea Turtle is the most colorful of the world's sea turtles, with an intricately mottled pattern of rich reddish or dark brown, orange, and yellow markings on each scute of its carapace. The keeled carapace is bony with large, overlapping scutes, elliptical in shape, and with four costal

Eretmochelys imbricata, Maldives Islands. Photo by Dan Herschman.

Eretmochelys imbricata, Maldives Islands. Photo by Carl Buttner.

scutes. The head possesses two pairs of prefrontal scales, and the jaw is not serrated but instead has a hawk-like beak. Each flipper has two claws. Hatchlings are brown with pale blotches on their scutes, and the carapaces possess two ridges. The plastron of the male is slightly concave, aiding in copulation by allowing him to more closely "ride" the female's carapace during copulation.

SIMILAR SPECIES The Green Sea Turtle (*Chelonia mydas*) is larger and has only one pair of prefrontal scales on its head. The carapace of the Green Sea Turtle is a more uniform coloration, lacking the rich mottled colors, and the scutes do not overlap. The Loggerhead Sea Turtle (*Caretta caretta*) is also larger and, although it is a similar reddish-brown color, it possesses five or more costal scutes on each side of the carapace. The Kemp's Ridley Sea Turtle (*Lepidochelys kempii*) is smaller, more uniformly colored, and also has five or more costal scutes on each side of the carapace, the first of which is in contact with the nuchal scute.

DISTRIBUTION The Hawksbill Sea Turtle occurs throughout tropical waters of all the world's oceans. It is infrequently encountered in the Gulf of Mexico and has been recorded from seven of Texas' coastal counties (Galveston, Calhoun, Aransas, Nueces, Kleberg, Willacy, and Cameron). Most of these records reflect dead specimens found washed up on Texas beaches.

NATURAL HISTORY This species occurs primarily along coastal reefs, rocky areas, estuaries, and lagoons in tropical and sub-tropical seas. Its diet includes sponges, anemones, squid, and shrimp. Hatchlings spend considerable time floating among rafts of sargassum, where the carapace patterns presumably provide camouflage from avian predators.

REPRODUCTION Females come ashore to nest every 2–4 years and may nest 3–6 times per nesting season. From 50–160 eggs are laid per nest. The spherical eggs take 60 days to incubate on average. Mating takes place in shallow waters near shore.

COMMENTS AND CONSERVATION The Hawksbill Sea Turtle is considered to be critically endangered internationally and is protected in the United States by both state and federal agencies. These turtles are harvested for their meat and shells, the scutes of which are used to make "tortoise shell" jewelry, hair ornaments, and other decorative items. Travelers to the Caribbean (and other tropical locales) should be aware that these items are frequently sold in local markets. Such items will be confiscated by US customs when re-entering the United States.

Kemp's Ridley Sea Turtle
Lepidochelys kempii
(Garman, 1880)

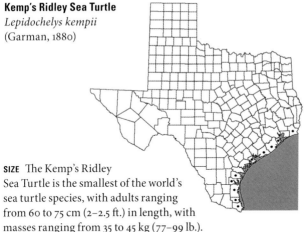

SIZE The Kemp's Ridley
Sea Turtle is the smallest of the world's
sea turtle species, with adults ranging
from 60 to 75 cm (2–2.5 ft.) in length, with
masses ranging from 35 to 45 kg (77–99 lb.).

DESCRIPTION The carapace is wide and heart shaped with a mid-dorsal keel. The scutes are gray in color but may appear olive green in older adults. The plastron scutes are white to yellowish. Five costal scutes are present, with the first touching the nuchal scute. On the bridge between the carapace and plastron, four scutes are present, each with a distinct pore. There are two pairs of prefrontal scales on the head.

Lepidochelys kempii, adult, Kleberg Co., Texas. Photo by Sal Scibetta.

Lepidochelys kempii, adult, Kleberg Co., Texas. Photo by Sal Scibetta.

Young and hatchling turtles possess three ridges on the dark gray carapace and four on the pale plastron. There is a dark gray streak on the rear edge of each flipper.

In males, the tail extends well beyond the rear margin of the carapace. There is also a thick, curved claw on the forelimb (flipper).

SIMILAR SPECIES The larger Loggerhead Sea Turtle (*Caretta caretta*) is reddish brown in color and lacks an interanal scute; three or four of the bridge scutes lack pores. The Hawksbill Turtle (*Eretmochelys imbricata*) is more colorful, possessing an intricate pattern of brown and orange streaks on each scute. Neither the Hawksbill nor Green Turtle (*Chelonia mydas*) possess nuchal scutes in contact with the first costal.

DISTRIBUTION The Kemp's Ridley is a turtle of the western Atlantic and Gulf of Mexico. In summers it may be found in the Gulf Stream current as far north as New England. Its primary nesting ground is on the coast of Tamaulipas, Mexico, along a 26 km (16 mi.) stretch of beach at Playa de Rancho Nuevo. Efforts to establish a second nesting colony on protected beaches of Texas' Padre Island National Seashore have been successful, although only a few turtles nest there annually. This species has been documented from 11 of Texas' coastal counties, both from carcasses found washed ashore and sightings of live turtles in coastal waters.

NATURAL HISTORY The Kemp's Ridley is an inhabitant primarily of shallow coastal waters. Young turtles may use floating mats of sargassum as refuges until they attain sufficient size to avoid most predators (usually for 2 years). The diet of these turtles primarily includes marine invertebrates, including crabs, shrimp, clams, mussels, and sea urchins. Although they are primarily carnivorous, plant material may also be consumed.

REPRODUCTION Kemp's Ridleys nest from April to July during the daytime. Females come ashore en masse in synchronized groups known as *arribadas*. Each female comes ashore to lay 100–110 eggs per clutch, 2–3 times each season. Most females nest every 2 years, with some individuals nesting annually and others nesting every third year. Females have been shown to return to the same beaches from which they were hatched. This feature of their nesting has allowed conservation biologists to

Lepidochelys kempii, hatchling, Kleberg Co., Texas. Photo by Sal Scibetta.

imprint hatchling turtles on South Texas beaches in order to establish a second nesting site for the species. Eggs average 39 mm (1.5 in.) in diameter and take 70 days to hatch. Nest predators include ghost crabs, grackles, vultures, coyotes, raccoons, skunks, and humans.

COMMENTS AND CONSERVATION   The Kemp's Ridley was almost driven to extinction between the 1940s and 1970s, primarily from robbing nests for eggs (for human consumption), from killing nesting females for food, and from incidental take in shrimp boat nets. It is considered an endangered species by both state and federal agencies. The United States and Mexico are coordinating on a recovery project called the Kempii Project. Although nesting beaches are now protected and nest raiding and the killing of nesting females are illegal, beach development remains a problem. Efforts to protect this turtle include the establishment of a second nesting colony on the Padre Island National Seashore, "head-starting" sea turtles by rearing them in captivity until they reach a size large enough to reduce their risk of predation, and the passage of laws requiring the use of TEDs on shrimp boat nets. Although TEDs are widely used in US waters, their efficiency at protecting turtles from becoming entrapped and drowned in shrimp nets remains unclear as there are still numbers of dead sea turtles (of several species) found washed ashore on Texas beaches each year.

FAMILY: DERMATOCHELYIDAE

This family is represented by a single living species, the Leatherback Sea Turtle (*Dermochelys coriacea*). It is the largest living turtle and ranges widely throughout the world's oceans in tropical, subtropical, and warm temperate waters. Unlike the hard-shelled sea turtles, its carapace lacks hardened scutes and is instead covered with a leathery skin ridged with seven prominent keels.

Leatherback Sea Turtle
Dermochelys coriacea
(Vandelli, 1761)

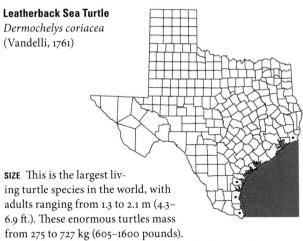

SIZE This is the largest living turtle species in the world, with adults ranging from 1.3 to 2.1 m (4.3–6.9 ft.). These enormous turtles mass from 275 to 727 kg (605–1600 pounds).

DESCRIPTION These turtles lack a bony shell covered in scutes and instead possess a largely cartilaginous shell with a matrix of hexagonal bones embedded within it. The shell is narrowly triangular in shape, with the apex at the caudal end. The shell is prominently keeled, with one keel down the center and three more on each side. The skin covering the shell is black, blue black, or very dark brown and is spotted with small, irregular white marks. As with all sea turtles, the front legs are modified

Dermochelys coriacea, adult, Playa Grande, Costa Rica. Photo by William B. Montgomery.

Dermochelys coriacea, hatchling, Guerrero, Mexico. Photo by William Mertz.

into flippers and are particularly large in this species. The flippers lack claws. The head appears to be relatively small in comparison with the body, and the upper jaw is deeply notched with two cusps. Hatchlings are lighter in color than adults and have the flippers broadly edged in white.

SIMILAR SPECIES The Leatherback Sea Turtle is unique and unmistakable. All other sea turtles have bony scutes and claws.

DISTRIBUTION The Leatherback Sea Turtle ranges across all the world's oceans in tropical and subtropical areas. It is infrequently encountered in the Gulf of Mexico. It has been recorded from seven Texas counties (Jefferson, Galveston, Brazoria, Aransas, Nueces, Kennedy, and Cameron). These records primarily reflect specimens found dead and washed ashore.

NATURAL HISTORY This species is a highly migratory pelagic species of deep ocean waters that feeds primarily on jellyfish. Its body is well insulated with fat to aid it in maintaining its body temperature when it dives in search of its prey. Adults have few natural predators.

REPRODUCTION These giant turtles nest in December of each year, and, depending on region of nesting, each female lays from 6 to 7 clutches of 50–180 billiard-ball-sized eggs. Eggs are laid approximately 1 m (3.3 ft.) deep on sandy beaches. Nests are raided by a variety of predators, including ghost crabs, gulls, a variety of shorebirds (including turnstones, knots, and plovers), vultures, crows, opossums, raccoons, feral dogs and pigs, and, in some parts of the world, humans.

Young take approximately 65 days to hatch. After they emerge from their nest, they make a perilous journey across the nesting beach to the sea, where they are subject to predation from gulls, crows, frigate birds, and ghost crabs. Upon reaching the surf, they face continued danger from birds and a variety of fish, sharks, and octopi.

COMMENTS AND CONSERVATION The Leatherback Sea Turtle is considered an endangered species at both the federal and state level. Threats to this species include longline fishing and open-water trawling with seine or purse nets. Floating plastic bags pose a unique threat to this species when they are mistakenly ingested by the great turtles—floating plastic bags bear a marked similarity to the turtle's natural prey of jellyfish.

In the past, the turtles were slaughtered for meat and for their oils, which were used in cosmetics. Nests were raided and eggs taken for human consumption—a practice that is now illegal but which may still occur in some impoverished areas.

CLASS CROCODILIA

The Crocodilia were formerly considered to be a member of the class Reptilia along with turtles, lizards, snakes, amphisbaenians, and the tuatara. However, the exclusion of birds from the class Reptilia rendered this group paraphyletic (meaning the group did not include all descendants of a single common ancestor). In order to rectify this situation, the class Reptilia is now used to refer specifically to the group of living vertebrates that includes the lizards, snakes, amphisbaenians, and the tuatara, whereas the turtles are placed in the class Chelonia, the crocodilians are placed in the class Crocodilia, and the birds remain in the class Aves. Although dissimilar in habits and morphology, birds and crocodilians are each other's nearest living relatives. Crocodilians range in adult size from 1.2 m to nearly 7 m (3.9–23 ft.). All living crocodilians are aquatic predators that feed primarily on vertebrates as adults. There are 25 living species of crocodilian in the world, primarily in tropical regions. Two species occur naturally in the United States north of Mexico, with a third species having been introduced in Florida. A single species occurs naturally in Texas.

FAMILY: ALLIGATORIDAE

The family Alligatoridae includes eight species distributed primarily across the New World tropics, with a single species occurring in warm temperate regions of China and another occurring in the southeastern coastal plains of the United States. Compared with crocodiles, the Alligatoridae have broader snouts and feed less upon terrestrial prey. A single species occurs naturally north of Mexico, with a second species having been introduced in southern Florida. Only the American Alligator (*Alligator mississippiensis*) occurs naturally in Texas.

American Alligator
Alligator mississippiensis
(Daudin, 1803)

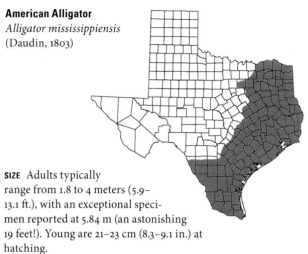

SIZE Adults typically range from 1.8 to 4 meters (5.9–13.1 ft.), with an exceptional specimen reported at 5.84 m (an astonishing 19 feet!). Young are 21–23 cm (8.3–9.1 in.) at hatching.

DESCRIPTION The American Alligator has the appearance of a huge, scaly lizard with four distinct limbs and a long, dorsoventrally flattened tail. Adults are dark gray or black with faint banding—traces of the juvenile pattern—present in some smaller specimens, particularly on the tail. Hatchlings and small juveniles possess bold yellow crossbands on a black back-

Alligator mississippiensis, Monroe Co., Florida.

Alligator mississippiensis, Chambers Co., Texas.

ground, both on the body and the flanks and tail. The feet are slightly webbed. Each of the body scales is relatively large and is supported by bones called osteoderms, which serve the animal much like an articulated suit of armor. The American Alligator possesses a broad, rounded snout. Most of the teeth of the lower jaw, including the enlarged fourth tooth, fit into sockets present in the upper jaw. The nostrils are valved and close underwater. A nictitating membrane is present over the eyes, allowing the animal to see underwater.

SIMILAR SPECIES The American Alligator is Texas' only native crocodilian. It can be distinguished from the Spectacled Caiman (*Caiman crocodilus*), which is occasionally reported as an escaped "pet," by the caiman's smaller size, narrower snout, and the curved, bony, crosswise ridge present just in front of and between the eyes. Where the American Alligator co-occurs with the American Crocodile (*Crocodylus acutus*) in Florida, the American Crocodile can be distinguished by its much narrower snout, pattern of dark crossbands on a tan or olive background, and the enlarged fourth tooth of the lower jaw that is exposed rather than fitted into a socket in the upper jaw.

DISTRIBUTION The American Alligator ranges along the southeastern coastal plain from North Carolina to Texas, with populations extending northward into Arkansas along the Mississippi River. In Texas it occurs throughout the southeastern portion of the state, from the Red River northeast of the Dallas–Fort Worth metropolitan area south along the eastern edge of the Balcones Escarpment and into the Tamaulipan Thornscrub south of San Antonio. It occurs in the following watersheds: Mississippi, Sabine, Neches, Trinity, Brazos, Colorado, Guadalupe, Nueces, and Rio Grande.

NATURAL HISTORY The American Alligator is most abundant in coastal marshes, lakes, bayous, and swamps associated with larger rivers. It prefers still and quiet waters. In larger reservoirs it typically frequents the backwaters of quiet bays lined with aquatic vegetation such as cattails and lily pads. Although it can tolerate saltwater for short periods of time, it is not considered to be marine. Brackish waters of coastal swamps are tolerated but not preferred, and it will be most abundant in the freshwater marshes just inland from brackish estuaries. Upstream, American Alligator populations are typically less dense, as the amount of available habitat decreases as one moves away from the immediate coast. The American Alligator's distribution stops when the muddy river bottoms are replaced by rocky substrates, which prevent burrowing.

The American Alligator is a very opportunistic feeder, preying on all manner of vertebrate and crustacean life that it may encounter, including fish, lizards, snakes, turtles, mammals, waterfowl, and crayfish. Average prey size is correlated with size of the individual, with larger animals taking larger prey. Mammals most commonly included in their diet are nutria, raccoons, opossums, and beaver; however, feral hogs and white-tailed deer may be taken as prey by larger specimens.

The American Alligator is a keystone species in many marsh ecosystems, as it digs holes that retain water during droughts. These holes are often enlarged throughout the life of the animal and may result in substantial impoundments of water persisting in the driest of seasons. These "gator holes" provide important refuges for all manner of aquatic life, including invertebrates, fish, amphibians, turtles, reptiles, birds, and mammals.

American Alligators may frequently be observed basking, particularly early in the morning or late in the evening. Although their behavior cycles are temperature dependent, they show a distinct nocturnal tendency, spending a great deal of

Alligator mississippiensis, juveniles, Collier Co., Florida.

time sleeping or resting during the day and actively foraging at night.

VOICE Male American Alligators give a throaty, bellowing roar during breeding season in order to attract mates and establish territories. Males may also vigorously and loudly slap the surface of the water with their tails. Females also vocalize and may roar like males but never as loudly. When calling to their young, female alligators grunt, sounding much like a pig. Hatchling and young alligators produce a high-pitched moaning grunt or chirp, particularly when in distress—a sound that is sure to attract the attention of an attentive and defensive mother.

REPRODUCTION Female American Alligators build nests composed of large mounds of vegetable debris 1–2 m (3.3–6.6 ft.) in diameter and 45–90 cm (17.7–35.4 in.) high. This nest is built in the spring. The females lay from 25 to 60 hard-shelled eggs measuring 7.6 cm (3 in.) in length. These eggs are buried in the center of the nest. Females guard and attend to their nests throughout the 9-week incubation period and may periodically add to or remove vegetation from the nest. At or just prior to hatching, the young begin to vocalize, and the female will uncover the eggs and carry the young to water in her mouth, usually one or two at a time.

COMMENTS AND CONSERVATION In the past, the American Alligator was relentlessly hunted for its hide and meat; it was also persecuted as a potential predator on livestock. Populations of American Alligators were so dramatically reduced that it was designated as a federally endangered species in 1967. Complete protection of this species from hunting and persecution allowed this prolific species to make a rapid and dramatic recovery, and it was removed from the endangered species list in 1987. Its range now includes most if not all of the area in which it occurred prior to overhunting. Today, populations of American Alligators may be hunted in Texas for both hide and meat under strict regulations established by the TPWD. See the TPWD website for details, as these regulations may change from year to year.

APPENDIX A

Species with Prehistoric Occurrence in Texas

Bolson Tortoise

Gopherus flavomarginatus Legler, 1959

Although now restricted to the Bolsón de Mapimí of southeastern Chihuahua, southwestern Coahuila, and northeastern Durango, fossil evidence suggests that the Bolson Tortoise inhabited much of the American Southwest during late Pleistocene and early Holocene times, including parts of the Chihuahuan Desert of West Texas. It is a large tortoise, with adults reaching 37 cm (14.6 in.) across the carapace. In coloration it is a straw-colored or yellowish tortoise, with each scute dark centered. The oblong carapace is low arched and flat topped in profile. The plastron is yellowish with a dark blotch on each scute that fades with age. The skin of the head, legs, and tail ranges from yellow to brown. The forelimbs are armored with large, overlapping scales, and the hind limbs are elephantine.

The Bolson Tortoise was not discovered by scientists until the 1950s, and it is currently restricted to an internally drained

Gopherus flavomarginatus, adult, captive specimen. Photo by Bill Love, Blue Chameleon Ventures.

desert grassland basin in northern Mexico at elevations between 1000–1300 m (3280–4265 ft.), where fewer than 10,000 tortoises are estimated to remain. Formerly this species was threatened by subsistence hunting and eaten widely by ranchers and farmers in the region. It is now protected from such harvest but remains threatened by desertification of its native grasslands and by brush clearing for agriculture.

The Bolson Tortoise was one of the first species proposed to be reintroduced into the American Southwest as part of the Pleistocene rewilding initiative. At the end of the Pleistocene, much of North America's megafauna (mammoths, lions, cheetah, ground sloths, and several species of bison) became extinct, possibly at the hands of Paleolithic hunters. This has resulted in unstable ecological communities throughout the region, as communities that have evolved under the influence of large mammals have been altered with their extinction. Advocates of Pleistocene rewilding suggest that descendants of this megafauna or their close ecological equivalents should be reintroduced into the American Southwest in order to stabilize these ecological communities as well as to provide safe havens for species endangered in their native ranges (such as elephants and lions).

Because the Bolson Tortoise occurred in the American Southwest until recent Holocene times, and because it is still present in the Chihuahuan Desert, reintroduction of this species into the American Southwest has been one of the first steps in the Pleistocene rewilding program. Currently, efforts are underway to establish populations of this species on private lands in New Mexico. It has also been proposed that populations of this species be established in protected areas in Texas, including Big Bend National Park.

Geochelone sulcata, adult, captive specimen. Photograph by Michael Price.

Geochelone sulcata, juvenile, captive specimen. Photograph by Michael Price.

APPENDIX B

Nonestablished Exotic Species

African Spurred Tortoise
Geochelone sulcata (Miller, 1779)

The African Spurred Tortoise is the third largest tortoise species in the world and the largest species not restricted to an island archipelago. Adults range from 60 to 90 cm (23.6–35.4 in.) across the carapace and may mass as much as 90 kg (198 lb.). The carapace is a yellowish-tan color, with darker margins for each scute. Concentric growth rings are prominent on each scute, the centers of which are slightly elevated in a pyramidal fashion. The forelimbs are armored with large scales, and the thighs possess prominent spurs. The species is native to Africa in the Sahara Desert and Sahel region of semiarid grassland and thornscrub bordering the Sahara to the south.

The African Spurred Tortoise is very popular in the pet trade. However, owing to its large size and digging ability, African Spurred Tortoises frequently escape backyard enclosures and commonly turn up on reptile rescue calls in urban and sub-

Caiman crocodilus, Iquitos, Peru. Photo by Mike Pingleton.

Caiman crocodilus, hatchling, Loreto Province, Peru. Photo by Kenneth P. Wray.

urban settings in Texas. Most such escapees are juveniles and young adults.

Spectacled Caiman
Caiman crocodilus (Linnaeus, 1758)

The Spectacled Caiman is native to Central and South America from southern Mexico to Argentina. It is smaller than the native American Alligator (*Alligator mississippiensis*), with adults ranging from 1.1 to 2.6 m (3.6–8.5 ft.) in length. Its ground color is greenish gray with darker crossbands. Its snout is narrower than that of the American Alligator, and a bony ridge forms a semicircle between the eyes much like the bridge in a pair of glasses.

Formerly, hatchling Spectacled Caimans were widely sold in the pet trade. As these animals outgrew their owners' ability to maintain them in home enclosures, some unscrupulous keepers released them into the wild in Texas. None of these releases have resulted in the establishment of breeding populations in Texas, although breeding populations have become established in Florida. Although no breeding populations are known to occur in Texas, Spectacled Caimans still turn up from time to time on reptile rescue calls in urban and suburban areas.

APPENDIX C

Table of Texas Turtles and Crocodilians and River Drainages They Inhabit

In the table below, we present a quick reference guide to the turtles of Texas and the river drainages that they inhabit. Species that are not associated with river drainages are indicated by the columns marked terrestrial, ponds and lakes, coastal estuaries, and marine.

SPECIES	TERRESTRIAL	PONDS AND LAKES	COASTAL ESTUARIES	MARINE	MISSISSIPPI–CANADIAN	MISSISSIPPI–RED	SABINE–NECHES	TRINITY	BRAZOS	COLORADO	GUADALUPE	NUECES	RIO GRANDE
Snapping Turtle (*Chelydra serpentina*)		●	●		●	●	●	●	●	●	●	●	●
Alligator Snapping Turtle (*Macrochelys temminckii*)					●	●	●						

(*continued*)

SPECIES	TERRESTRIAL	PONDS AND LAKES	COASTAL ESTUARIES	MARINE	MISSISSIPPI–CANADIAN	MISSISSIPPI–RED	SABINE–NECHES	TRINITY	BRAZOS	COLORADO	GUADALUPE	NUECES	RIO GRANDE
Cagle's Map Turtle (*Graptemys caglei*)											•		
Ouachita Map Turtle (*Graptemys ouachitensis*)					•								
Sabine Map Turtle (*Graptemys sabinensis*)							•						
False Map Turtle (*Graptemys pseudogeographica*)					•	•	•	•					
Texas Map Turtle (*Graptemys versa*)											•		
Diamond-backed Terrapin (*Malaclemys terrapin*)			•										
River Cooter (*Pseudemys concinna*)		•			•	•	•	•					
Rio Grande Cooter (*Pseudemys gorzugi*)		•											•
Texas River Cooter (*Pseudemys texana*)		•								•	•	•	•
Florida Red-bellied Cooter (*Pseudemys nelsoni*)		•									•		
Painted Turtle (*Chrysemys picta*)		•			•	•							•

236

SPECIES	TERRESTRIAL	PONDS AND LAKES	COASTAL ESTUARIES	MARINE	MISSISSIPPI–CANADIAN	MISSISSIPPI–RED	SABINE–NECHES	TRINITY	BRAZOS	COLORADO	GUADALUPE	NUECES	RIO GRANDE
Mexican Plateau Slider (*Trachemys gaigeae*)													•
Pond Slider (*Trachemys scripta*)		•	•		•	•	•	•	•	•	•	•	•
Chicken Turtle (*Deirochelys reticularia*)		•				•	•	•	•	•			
Eastern Box Turtle (*Terrapene carolina*)	•												
Ornate Box Turtle (*Terrapene ornata*)	•												
Texas Tortoise (*Gopherus berlandieri*)	•												
Smooth Softshell (*Apalone mutica*)					•	•	•	•	•	•			
Spiny Softshell (*Apalone spinifera*)		•			•	•	•	•	•	•	•	•	•
Yellow Mud Turtle (*Kinosternon flavescens*)		•	•		•	•	•	•	•	•	•	•	•
Rough-footed Mud Turtle (*Kinosternon hirtipes*)		•											•
Eastern Mud Turtle (*Kinosternon subrubrum*)		•	•			•	•	•	•	•	•	•	

(*continued*)

SPECIES	TERRESTRIAL	PONDS AND LAKES	COASTAL ESTUARIES	MARINE	MISSISSIPPI–CANADIAN	MISSISSIPPI–RED	SABINE–NECHES	TRINITY	BRAZOS	COLORADO	GUADALUPE	NUECES	RIO GRANDE
Razor-backed Musk Turtle (*Sternotherus carinatus*)		•				•	•	•	•				
Stinkpot (*Sternotherus odoratus*)		•				•	•	•	•	•	•	•	•
Loggerhead Sea Turtle (*Caretta caretta*)				•									
Green Sea Turtle (*Chelonia mydas*)				•									
Hawksbill Sea Turtle (*Eretmochelys imbricata*)				•									
Kemp's Ridley Sea Turtle (*Lepidochelys kempii*)				•									
Leatherback Sea Turtle (*Dermochelys coriacea*)				•									
American Alligator (*Alligator mississippiensis*)	•	•				•	•	•	•	•	•	•	•

APPENDIX D

Turtle and Crocodilian Informational Resources

TEXAS SOCIETIES

Herpetological societies provide a venue for those interested in reptiles and amphibians to interact with others that share their interests as well as to further their knowledge of reptiles and amphibians.

Texas Herpetological Society
East Texas Herpetological Society
Gulf Coast Turtle and Tortoise Society
Austin Herpetological Society
Brazos Valley Herpetological Society
Dallas–Fort Worth Herpetological Society
DFW Turtle & Tortoise Club
South Texas Herpetology Association
West Texas Herpetological Society

INTERNATIONAL US-BASED SOCIETIES

Most international societies focus either on conservation of or scientific research involving reptiles and amphibians and thus are often considered to be professional organizations.

American Society of Ichthyologists and Herpetologists (ASIH): publisher of the journal *Copeia*

The Herpetologists' League (HL): publisher of the journals *Herpetologica* and *Herpetological Monographs*

Society for the Study of Amphibians and Reptiles (SSAR): publisher of the journals *Journal of Herpetology, Herpetological Review,* and *Catalogue of American Amphibians and Reptiles*

Partners in Amphibian and Reptile Conservation (PARC)

Turtle Survival Alliance (TSA) (www.turtlesurvival.org)

TEXAS MUSEUMS

Research museums maintain collections of reptile and amphibian specimens that serve as a physical record of the history and distribution of reptile and amphibian populations. Specimens from these museums are often loaned to researchers across the country for examination in research projects.

Biodiversity Research and Teaching Collections (BRTC) at Texas A&M University (the BRTC was long referred to as the Texas Cooperative Wildlife Collection, and the initialism TCWC is still widely used both outside the museum and within the museum in its specimen catalog)

Texas Natural Heritage Collection (TNHC), maintained by the Texas Natural Science Center at the University of Texas at Austin

Amphibian and Reptile Diversity Research Center at the University of Texas at Arlington

WEBSITES

Distinguishing sites on the internet that provide quality information from those that are suspect presents a daunting challenge. The following sites are all associated with and maintained by professional herpetologists.

The Reptile Database (http://www.reptile-database.org)
Work is supported by the European Molecular Biology Laboratory (EMBL), Meyerhofstr. 1, D-69117 Heidelberg, Germany.

Animal Diversity Web (http://animaldiversity.org)
Work is supported by the National Science Foundation and the International Union for Conservation of Nature Crocodile Specialist Group (http://iucncsg.org).

Herps of Texas (http://www.zo.utexas.edu/research/txherps/)
Work is supported by the Natural Science Center at The University of Texas at Austin.

Texas Turtles (http://www.TexasTurtles.org).
Chelonian Research Foundation (http://www.chelonian.org).

CITIZEN SCIENCE PROJECTS

In recent years wildlife agencies across the country have sought to utilize the vast pool of volunteers that private citizens represent by establishing citizen science projects.

The BRTC/TCWC, the TNHC, and the TPWD have started a web-based vouchering system for observations using photographs that are taken by the public. These observations can be uploaded into the Herps of Texas Project (http://www.inaturalist.org/projects/herps-of-texas) and then used to help determine current distributions of our Texas turtles and crocodilians.

APPENDIX E

Map of Texas Counties

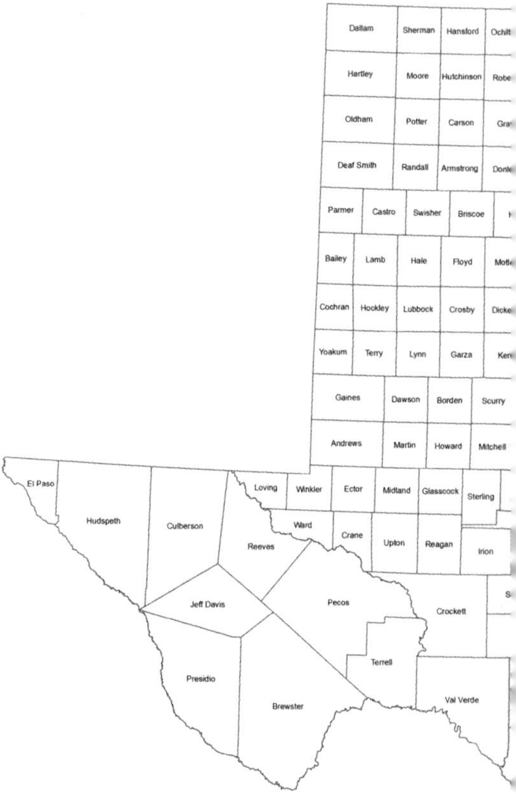

Map of Texas counties.

GLOSSARY

ABDOMINAL SCUTES Paired scutes on the plastron of a turtle posterior to the pectoral scutes.

ALLANTOIS A membrane in the amniotic egg that serves to contain metabolic wastes produced by the developing embryo.

AMMONIA A toxic metabolic waste produced through the breakdown of proteins; it must be eliminated from the bloodstream by excreting it into the surrounding water or by converting it to a less-toxic form such as urea or uric acid.

AMNION A membrane in the amniotic egg that encloses and protects the developing embryo.

AMNIOTE Group of tetrapod vertebrates that lay amniotic eggs or give birth to live young with nourishment membranes derived from those of the amniotic egg.

AMNIOTIC EGG Shelled eggs that contain the following internal membranes surrounding the embryo—the amnion, the chorion, the allantois, and the yolk sac.

AMPHISBAENIAN Burrowing reptiles variously regarded as close lizard relatives or as highly specialized lizards, typically possessing very short tails, lacking eyes or possessing small, nonfocusing eyes embedded within the skin, and having scales arranged as annuli encircling the body.

ANAPSID Group of tetrapod vertebrates in which the dermal roof of the skull is lacking in temporal openings, possibly including turtles.

ANIMALIA Heterotrophic multicellular eukaryotes lacking cell walls.

ARCHOSAUR/ARCHOSAURIA "Ruling Reptiles"; group of tetrapod vertebrates including crocodilians, the extinct dinosaurs and pterodactyls, and birds.

BARBEL A fleshy extension of the skin.

BASKING The act of laying in sunlight and absorbing heat energy.

CARAPACE Dorsal portion of the shell of a turtle.

CHELONIA The class that includes the turtles.

CHORDATA Group of animals that possess a flexible rod of cartilage down their backs (the notochord) at some time in their lives; includes vertebrates (in which the notochord is replaced by the bones of the spine) and invertebrate relatives.

CHORION A membrane in the amniotic egg that lies directly beneath the egg shell and allows the exchange of respiratory gases between the embryo and the outside environment.

CLOACA (PLURAL: CLOACAE) The common orifice into which the digestive, urinary, and reproductive tracts discharge their contents.

COPULATION A sexual process in which the male of the species inserts sperm into the female's cloaca to fertilize eggs.

COSTAL SCUTES A series of scutes on the flanks of a turtle's carapace, referred to as pleurals or laterals in some texts.

CRYPTODIRA Group or order of turtles that can withdraw their heads and necks directly rearward under their carapace.

DIAPSID Group of tetrapod vertebrates that possess two openings in the lateral portion of the dermal roof of the skull behind the eye. Includes living reptiles, crocodilians, and birds.

DIURNAL Active during the daylight.

ECTOTHERMIC An organism that is dependent on an external heat source to warm its body.

ENDEMIC Being unique to a particular geographic area.

ENDEMISM The ecological state of being unique to a particular geographic area.

EUKARYA Organisms that possess cells with a nucleus and membrane-bound organelles.

EUSUCHIA Group that includes modern crocodilians and their extinct ancestors.

GENERALIST A species that is able to exploit a wide variety of foods and (or) habitats.

GULAR Pertaining to the neck.

IN SITU Latin phrase meaning "in the original position," usually meant to indicate that the animal has been observed or photographed without disturbance.

KERATIN Protein that makes up the scutes and scales of turtles, crocodilians, reptiles, and birds; also makes up most of an animal's epidermis; includes feathers of birds, hair in mammals, and claws and fingernails.

LEPIDOSAURIA Group of diapsid "reptiles" with bodies covered in small scales, including the modern Reptilia along with extinct mosasaurs and ichthyosaurs.

MARGINAL SCUTES A series of scutes marking the lateral borders of the carapace.

MESOSUCHIA A group of extinct crocodilians known for both terrestrial and marine forms.

MONOPHYLETIC A condition in which a named taxon includes all descendants of a single common ancestor.

NOCTURNAL Active at night.

NUCHAL Pertaining to the back of the neck; scute present above the neck, sometimes referred to as the cervical.

PECTORAL SCUTE Scute present on the plastron of a turtle in the upper chest area.

PHYLOGENETIC SYSTEMATICS The field of biology that uses the characteristics of organisms—including morphological, behavioral, and genetic features—to infer the relationships among populations within species of organisms, among different species of organisms, or among groups of organisms described by higher taxonomic categories, such as families or orders.

PLASTRON The ventral half of a turtle's shell.

PLEURODIRA Group or order of turtles in which the head withdraws under the shell in a sideways manner.

POSTOCULAR Area immediately behind the eye.

PREFRONTAL SCALES Scales present on the forehead of a turtle.

PROTOSUCHIA A group containing the earliest known fossil crocodilians.

REPTILIA Formerly, a group of vertebrate organisms including turtles, crocodilians, lizards, snakes, amphisbaenians, and the tuatara; as currently understood, this group is restricted to the lizards, snakes, amphisbaenians, and the tuatara.

SCUTES Horny, scale-like plates of keratin covering the shell of most turtles.

SEPTUM Division between the two nostrils.

SPECIATION Process that gives rise to new species.

SPHENOSUCHIA A group of primitive fossil crocodilians.

SQUAMOSAL Bone present in the vertebrate skull behind and below the eye and above the articulation of the lower jaw.

SUPRAMARGINAL SCUTES Row of scutes present between the marginal and costal scutes in some turtles.

SUSTAINABILITY The capacity of a population or system to remain healthy, diverse, and productive over time, especially in the face of use or harvest of some of their members.

SYNAPSID Group of ancestral reptiles and their mammalian descendants possessing a single opening in the dermal roof of the skull between the temporal and squamosal bones.

TAXON (PLURAL: TAXA) The group of organisms united under a taxonomic name applied to that group of organisms.

TAXONOMY The field of biology that categorizes all living things into groups and assigns names to those groups.

TEMPORAL Region on the side of the head behind the eyes; alternatively, a bone present in the vertebrate skull behind the eye.

TETRAPOD Group of vertebrates possessing four limbs.

TUATARA A primitive, lizard-like reptile that inhabits islands off the coast of New Zealand.

TUBERCLE A small to large, rounded or triangular bump on the skin.

UREA A water-soluble form of nitrogenous waste; toxic ammonia is produced by cells as a by-product of the metabolism of proteins in cells. In aquatic organisms such as fish, ammonia may be excreted out of the bloodstream as it is produced, while in terrestrial organisms it is converted into less-toxic compounds such as urea, which is then disposed of as urine.

URIC ACID An insoluble form of nitrogenous waste found primarily in terrestrial, egg-laying organisms that is excreted as a whitish paste. Unlike urea (see above), the excretion of uric acid, although more metabolically expensive, wastes far less water and is commonly used by desert-adapted species.

VERTEBRAL SCUTES Row of scutes present along the midline of the carapace. Referred to as spinal scutes in some references.

YOLK OR YOLK SAC A membrane in the amniotic egg that encloses a reservoir of nutrients for the developing embryo.

BIBLIOGRAPHY

Behler, John L., and F. Wayne King. 1979. *The Audubon Society Field Guide to North American Reptiles and Amphibians*. New York: Alfred A. Knopf.

Conant, Roger, and Joseph T. Collins. 1998. *A Field Guide to Reptiles and Amphibians: Eastern and Central North America*. Peterson Field Guide Series 12. New York: Houghton Mifflin Company.

Dixon, James R. 2013. *Amphibians and Reptiles of Texas*, 3rd ed. College Station: Texas A&M Press.

Ernst, Carl H., and Roger W. Barbour. 1989. *Turtles of the World*. Washington, DC: Smithsonian Institution Press.

Ernst, Carl H., Jeffrey E. Lovich, and Roger W. Barbour. 1994. *Turtles of the United States and Canada*. Washington, DC: Smithsonian Institution Press.

International Union for Conservation of Nature Crocodile Specialist Group. 2014. http://iucncsg.org.

Lemos-Espinal, Julio A., and Hobart M. Smith. 2007. *Amphibians and Reptiles of the State of Chihuahua, Mexico*. Mexico City: Universidad Nacional Autónoma de México–Comisión Nacional para el Conocimiento y Uso de la Biodiversidad.

Lindeman, Peter V. 2013. *The Map Turtle and Sawback Atlas: Ecology, Evolution, and Distribution.* Norman, Oklahoma: University of Oklahoma Press.

Smith, Hobart M., and Edmund D. Brodie Jr. 1982. *A Guide to Field Identification of Reptiles of North America.* New York: Golden Press.

Texas State Historical Association. 2010. "Principal Rivers of Texas." *Texas Almanac.* http://www.texasalmanac.com/topics /environment/rivers.

Trauth, Stanley E., Henry W. Robison, and Michael V. Plummer. 2004. *The Amphibians and Reptiles of Arkansas.* Fayetteville, Arkansas: The University of Arkansas Press.

Uetz, Peter, and Jirí Hošek, eds. *The Reptile Database.* Accessed 2013; last modified December 2014. http://reptile-database.org.

Wermund, E. G. 1996. *River Basins of Texas.* Austin, Texas: Bureau of Economic Geology, University of Texas at Austin.

INDEX TO COMMON NAMES

Bold page numbers indicate detailed discussion

INDEX TO SCIENTIFIC NAMES